ST SWITHUN'S:

A Centenary History

St Swithun's
A Centenary History

Priscilla Bain

Phillimore

1984

Published by
PHILLIMORE & CO. LTD.
Shopwyke Hall, Chichester, Sussex

ISBN 0 85033 524 8

Printed and bound in Great Britain by
THE CAMELOT PRESS LTD.
Southampton, England

To the Staff and Pupils,
past and present,
of St Swithun's

Contents

List of Illustrations

(between pages 78 and 79)

List of Text Illustrations

drawn by *Nicola James*

Acknowledgements

In asking me to write the history of the first hundred years of St Swithun's, the Chairman and members of the Council have provided me with a fascinating opportunity to explore virtually the whole history of girls' independent education as we recognise the term today. For this I am very grateful to them, and for allowing me freedom of access to all the school records which still exist.

By her generous hospitality the present headmistress, Olwen Davies, has helped me to overcome the disadvantage of living 70 miles from my main source material, and both she and the Bursar and present members of the Staff have given me freely of that most precious of commodities in any school—their time. In particular, Pamela Johnston has acted as a vital link between me and the school and has been a source of much inspiration and encouragement and a most sympathetic and patient sounding-board during the process of composition.

The Art Department, too, needs special thanks for its enthusiastic help with the photographs and layout of the illustrations. Nick Richardson-White and John King have provided the modern photographs and the dust-cover has been designed and executed by Nick Richardson-White.

This book could not have been written in its present form without the help of past members of the school, both girls and staff. The Old Girls responded splendidly to pleas for memories of their school days, so much so that it is impossible to acknowledge them all by name. I hope they will feel it some reward to see themselves in print, even if anonymously. The photographs dug out from ancient albums have been a particular pleasure. I have had much help, too, from former members of staff; in particular Miss Havergal has provided a wealth of material for the period of the Second World War; Miss Hobson's memory extending over more than half the school's total history has been invaluable and Miss Snowball and Mrs. Claye have, too, been most generous in their help.

Miss Evans deserves special thanks for bearing with me through long periods of questions and discussions which did much to illuminate the period of her Headmistress-ship.

Two members of the present Winchester community, James Sabben-Clare, Second Master at Winchester College, and Barbara Carpenter Turner, the City's latest historian, have provided important information on personalities involved in the early years of the school's life, and members of the Bramston family, in particular Robert Beloe and Jock Luard have been most kind in giving me access to the Bramston family papers now lodged with the Essex Record Office.

Much of the material relating to the setting up of the school in 1883 and 1884 comes from the *Hampshire Chronicle* and without its full reporting of all the important occasions in the school's life this history would be much more sparse.

The introductory chapter relies almost entirely on material drawn from Josephine Kamm's history of women's education *Hope Deferred* and I am grateful to her publishers, Macmillan and Co., for their permission to draw on it freely. I would like to thank, too, Mrs. Georgina Battiscombe and her publishers, Constable and Company Ltd., for permission to quote from her biography of Charlotte M. Yonge the account of the inauguration of the Charlotte Yonge Scholarship.

Finally, the unenviable task of putting my handwritten manuscript into typescript has fallen to Joan Foss and Olive Tucker, and I cannot thank them enough for their forbearance and expertise.

Introduction

During the second half of the 19th century, women's education underwent a revolution, and St Swithun's is a child of that revolution, one of many and one of the younger ones, but with the classic characteristics of the movement which may be summed up in a phrase used by its foundress 'sound learning and true religion'.

By the middle of the 19th century there were a number of determined and largely self-taught women who were no longer prepared to accept a belief in the inherent inferiority of the female intellect or the low standard of teaching available to them. With few exceptions, whether in schools run by National Societies, private schools, or at home taught by governesses, girls' education was either severely practical or laid more stress on 'accomplishments' than the training of the mind and systematic learning, and in all these spheres one of the main impediments to progress was the lack of any training or real education on the part of their teachers.

It was in an effort to remedy this that the first advance was made. The Governesses Benevolent Association was founded in 1843 primarily to work for better conditions of pay and employment and as some sort of refuge for the vast numbers of governesses who were the main source of education for girls of middle and upper class backgrounds. But in order to justify claims for better payment and treatment it was felt that governesses would first have to show that their own professional standards were worthy of consideration. For this purpose a series of evening lectures was arranged in the winter of 1847 by Rev. F. D. Maurice, Professor of English Literature at King's College, London, and one of the chief supporters of the Governesses Benevolent Association: these proved so popular that they were quickly supplemented by a parallel series during the day. It so happened that at the same time one of Queen Victoria's ladies-in-waiting was collecting money for the foundation of a college for women and realising the value of the lecture series gave the money both for the purpose of making the lectures permanent and for providing premises at which they could be given. A house in Harley Street next door to the Governesses Benevolent Institution was taken and in 1848 Queen's College for Women was opened.

Its courses were designed primarily for governesses and intending governesses to improve their standard of knowledge, but classes were from the beginning open to any 'lady' over 12 years of age and such was their popularity that very soon further divisions had to be made into junior and senior classes. Within six months a second college, Bedford, was founded and in 1850 Frances Mary Buss opened the North London Collegiate School which served as a model for all Girls' High Schools founded thereafter. In 1858 Dorothea Beale who had been one of the early pupils and subsequently a teacher at Queen's College, Harley Street, became Headmistress of Cheltenham Ladies College, which then became the pattern for many of the girls'

Public Schools. In all these establishments the acquisition of a sound body of knowledge by systematic teaching and learning was the prime object.

This is not the place to pursue the struggle for women to be admitted to public examinations and universities, but it is a fascinating story, and very well told in Josephine Kamm's *Hope Deferred* (Methuen, 1965) to whom I am indebted for most of the material in this introductory chapter.

Another great step forward was taken when the Schools' Inquiry Commission of 1864, set up mainly to investigate boys' Public Schools, was induced to include evidence from girls' schools, and among its recommendations was one that a girls' school organised on the lines of North London Collegiate be set up in every town of over 4,000 inhabitants. In order to help implement this proposal the Girls' Public Day School Society was formed in 1872 and opened its first schools in Chelsea and Notting Hill. Similar schools were opened in provincial cities such as Manchester and Leeds and some older foundations were re-organised to provide a like type of education, among them Haberdasher Askes, the Perse in Cambridge, Godolphin in Salisbury. The first of the boarding schools modelled on the lines of a boys' Public School was St Leonards at St Andrews, in 1877; Roedean followed in 1885 and Wycombe Abbey in 1896.

That Winchester gained a High School in 1884 is due to the inspiration of Anna Bramston, daughter of the then Dean of Winchester, John Bramston. She and her lifelong friend, Aimée LeRoy, were in their youth protegées of Charlotte M. Yonge the famous novelist, who herself was the disciple of John Keble, one of the progenitors of the Oxford movement. He became Vicar of Hursley, in 1835, in whose parish the village of Otterbourne, Miss Yonge's home, lay. As well as writing novels, Miss Yonge launched, in 1851, a magazine called *The Monthly Packet*, designed as a Church of England paper for young people, and through it built up a circle of admirers, among them Anna Bramston and Aimée LeRoy, who formed themselves into a society whose main object was the improvement of their minds. They asked Miss Yonge to be their president; she became 'Mother Goose', they were her goslings, and they published at intervals *The Barnacle*, a manuscript magazine. Among other members were girls from the Coleridge and Moberly families who contributed much to the early years of higher education for women, and though Miss Yonge herself was never deeply involved in the movement for the betterment of womens' education she nevertheless, as a famous and successful woman writer, had her links with it and gave her support to the Governesses Benevolent Association, though holding aloof from the main movement. George Moberly, who had become Headmaster of Winchester College in 1835, and who with his family probably became the young Charlotte Yonge's greatest friends, provided a link with the world of education as well as being a sympathiser with the Oxford Movement. When Anna Bramston's father became Dean in 1873 she was absorbed as a young woman into this society. There came into Winchester also other women active in the betterment of womens' status; Mary Sumner, the wife of George Sumner the Bishop of Guildford, resident in the Close, who was the foundress of the Mothers' Union and to whose magazine *Mothers in Council* Miss Yonge was a contributor, and Josephine Butler who, with her husband George Butler, from 1882 to 1890 a Canon of Winchester, had taken up the cause of homeless women and prostitutes when he was Headmaster of Liverpool College.

So it was, when Anna Bramston heard Miss Elizabeth Sewell, already well known as an authoress and an educationalist, speak on the desirability of establishing girls' High Schools in the Winchester Diocese she responded to Miss Sewell's prompting.

The practical approach and independent research are introduced early in our science syllabuses...

... And emphasis is laid on original and individual work

I
Beginnings

On Saturday 3 May 1884 the *Hampshire Chronicle* contained this paragraph:

Winchester High School for Girls

The school for which the names of 16 pupils are now entered, will be opened on Monday next. We understand that the subscribers and the parents of those children who will take advantage of it had an opportunity on Wednesday of seeing the classrooms and that those who had accepted this invitation of the Council of Management (numbering about 55) expressed great satisfaction at the arrangements. Besides the Mayor, the Venerable Archdeacon Atkinson, several other members of the Council and the Head Mistress (Miss Jurgensen) there were present the Very Reverend Dean Bramston and Mrs. Bramston, Mrs. Harold Browne, Canon and Mrs. Sumner, the Warden and Mrs. Lee, Captain and Mrs. B. Knight, the Rev. W. A. C. Chevalier, the Rev. H. C. Dickens, the Rev. W. Jeffrey Hills, T. C. Langdon, Esq., Mrs. Cotesworth, Messrs. W. Bailey, T. Lloyd, J. Pamplin, J. C. Parmiter, G. Pointer, W. Stopher, G. Ward, W. Warren and many ladies.

We believe that absence from Winchester alone prevented the Head Master of the College from coming but our readers may be interested to know that Mr. Fearon has lately taken a leading part in starting a similar school in Durham and that he has expressed great interest in the establishment of a High School in this city.

For those who are familiar with the leading personalities of Winchester in the late 19th century it is clear that the school which received its first 17 pupils on 5 May 1884 enjoyed a wide measure of support from the local community; the Cathedral, the College, the professions and the substantial business men of the town are all represented amongst those who visited the school in the week before it officially opened at what is now No. 17 Southgate Street.

Probably the first indication which the people of Winchester had of the intention to open a new school for girls was a short statement in the *Hampshire Chronicle* of 20 October 1883: 'It is proposed to establish in Winchester a superior day school for girls, with moderate fees, the scale being graduated according to age. If this scheme is carried out the Bishop of Winchester has consented to become its patron'. But we are fortunate in having an account of its origins written for the first issue of the school magazine *The Chronicle* in 1897 by Miss LeRoy. Although Miss LeRoy probably felt hesitant about stating it directly St Swithun's has always been clear that its effective founder was Miss Bramston and that it was her enthusiasm, capacity for organisation and determination which led to the formation of a committee of men and women sometime in 1883 for the purpose of providing a secondary education based on Christian principles for girls in Winchester and its neighbourhood. The early records of this committee, which later became the first School Council, have been lost, but they were evidently still in existence when Miss Finlay was writing the history of the school for its 50th Anniversary and she fortunately recorded the names of the committee, and quoted from the Minute Book. The first chairman was Archdeacon Atkinson, and the members of the committee were Rev. J.H.T. Du Boulay; Dr. Fearon (then the Headmaster of the College); Miss LeRoy; Rev. W. C. Streatfield; J. F. Kirby, Esq. (Bursar of the College); Canon Warburton; Mrs. Byrne; Miss Charlotte M. Yonge; Rev. A. J. Toye; Mrs. R. Moberly; and Miss Bramston (the Hon. Secretary from 1884 to 1930).

Miss LeRoy had this to say about the reasons for the foundation of the school:
It is always a pleasure to recall the beginning of anything about which we are interested. The readers of this first High School *Chronicle* will doubtless like to know how the idea of the High School at Winchester originated. Miss Sewell, who has for long been well known as the author Amy Herbert, having all her life taken much interest in education, spoke one day on the advisability of having good Church Boarding Schools in various towns of the Diocese. After much talk, however, it was thought that at any rate for Winchester a real high school would be a better plan, and Bishop Harold Browne, having been written to on the subject, replied 'I shall be most happy to give my countenance and support to the scheme'. Miss Buss, the great pioneer of the High School movement [and at that time Headmistress of the North London Collegiate School] also wrote encouraging words - 'I think there would be sure to be a Church High School wanted in Winchester'. Helped on by these cheering remarks a Council of Management was formed, and though the members of it were not all hopeful, and many of them were very ignorant about most essential things, they were happily for themselves ignorant of their ignorance, and braced by much cold water from their fellow citizens, they were quite ready to consider Miss Sewell's remark as prophetic when, first hearing of the scheme, she said 'Of course it will be uphill work at first, but I think there can be little doubt of ultimate success'.

Miss LeRoy went on to describe early discussions about the form the school should take. There were at that time existing several Day School Companies formed as a result of the tremendous impetus given to girls' education during the second half of the 19th century who might have been prepared to help establish a school in Winchester; but apparently one Company refused to consider founding a school in such a small place, and another stated that if it lent any money it would require supreme control in the school. So it was decided that the Council would proceed independently and attempt to raise the money necessary to begin by subscription. A Minute of Thursday 6 November 1883 recorded that so far there was only a possibility of nine pupils (and even this was shortly to dwindle to four) and of the £800 needed only £120 had been promised. Miss LeRoy went on:

Cast upon its own resources, the Council called a Public Meeting on January 25th 1884. The Bishop promised to come and speak, and Mrs. Harold Browne wrote these cheering words 'We will all put on rose-coloured spectacles, and by God's blessing this scheme will succeed. It is sure to be wanted in such a city as Winchester and fourteen or fifteen children will make a beginning and the snowball will soon grow into a full grown man'.

The *Hampshire Chronicle* printed a special supplement giving a very full report of the meeting, and it is perhaps worth quoting from the speeches as they give some indication of the social attitudes and views on women's education then prevailing. The Bishop of Winchester—Bishop Harold Browne—opening the meeting, felt that places of education was a great want of the present day, and one which Winchester would do well to think about, since it was not only 'an ancient and a royal city but a city famous for having been the first in England in which a public school was instituted—he thought he might venture to say that this school was at the top of the public schools of England (*applause*). Having among them such an admirable institution which had for five hundred years provided for the education of the boys of the higher and middle classes surely Winchester felt more than most places the need of a public school for girls in the same sphere of life (*hear, hear*). Women were the great educators of the world . . . there was not a man alive who did not feel that he was educated by his mother (*hear, hear*) and if women were to be the great educators they wanted a sound and solid education'.

After the Bishop's speech, the Rev. R. Wilde moved a resolution 'that this meeting is strongly impressed with the advantages to be gained by girls from education conducted on the High School system as it is now established in the principal towns in the country'. He went on to describe the advantages of High Schools in bringing different classes together and referred to the case of a tradesman in Portsmouth who could not obtain the education he desired for his child, the mistress of a school refusing to receive her because she was a tradesman's daughter; whereas in a High School the daughter of a peer and the daughter of a butcher might sit side by side.

Miss Westmacott, invited to speak as she was the headmistress of a school founded three years earlier near Eaton Square, developed this theme. 'At first people held aloof from us for fear of a "mixture", but, strange to say, this fear was entirely on the side of the tradespeople who thought we were too select for them! One mother, a draper's wife, hesitated for a whole year before she could resolve to send her little girl to us, so much did she dread the child's being looked down upon. But she has managed to overcome her scruples, and the child is now working quite happily with the rest. We have had, in close juxtaposition, the daughter of a marquis, and the daughter of an hotel-keeper'. She felt that school should be a republic in which everyone had equal rights. 'One of the great evils of small private schools is that the daughters of rich or titled parents are treated with a distinction by no means due to their own merits, and they naturally accept the position, and look down with contempt on those who are, from a social point of view, less favoured than, although in moral and intellectual qualities they may be superior to, themselves. This state of affairs is not possible in a large public school, where each girl stands or falls on her own merits, and there is no respect of persons'.

She went on to describe the more academic aspects of High School education and while she did not wish to decry in any way the work of the *good* private governess 'if I could give you any idea of the utter incompetency of the majority of governesses, both English and foreign, you would hardly believe me, but it is daily brought under my notice in the results of their teaching in the children who are sent to me. Again and again girls come to us, thirteen, fourteen or fifteen years of age, unable to write or spell, totally ignorant of the first principles of arithmetic, with the merest smattering of history, and if they profess a knowledge of French, it is nothing more than a little surface chatter, destitute of any substratum of grammar. If I could lay before you some of the examination papers done by the new girls, you would agree with me that the children of our upper and middle classes are often far less well taught than those who attend our National and Board schools'.

When discussing the widespread anxiety about overwork, Miss Westmacott described a situation which finds some echoes in schools today. She said that in some cases apparent overwork could result from homework being done in unsuitable surroundings, or not being properly regulated by parents. 'I remember one of my girls who was eager about her work, but whose mother never liked to refuse an invitation for her: the girl would come home from a dance at midnight and then be allowed to do her preparation until two in the morning'. The situation may still be a familiar one today, but the likelihood is that it would be the girl's own choice!

The work of the upper forms in Miss Westmacott's school was based on the syllabus of the Oxford and Cambridge Local Examination although girls were not compelled to take the examination. It was sometimes objected that so much intellectual work did not leave enough time for the acquirement of accomplishments. 'I only wish this were true! Anyone who has listened to the average performer on the pianoforte at musical evenings, penny readings, parish concerts and the like, must, I am sure, often feel tempted to say with me that it would be well if half our girls were not allowed to learn music at all'. She ended more seriously by urging, as the Bishop had, that a good education would make girls better mothers 'or else, if wifehood and motherhood are not to be their portion, they will equally need such training as will enable them to live noble and useful lives as unmarried women; not frittering away their time in gossip and purposeless occupation but spending and being spent for God and their neighbour'.

The meeting then turned to the practicalities of setting up a High School in Winchester, and a member of the Council of Management, the Rev. J.H. du Boulay, proposed that an initial sum of £800 by subscription would be necessary to found the school. If they could obtain 15 pupils in the first year, 30 in the second and 60 in the third, the £800 could be repaid at the end of five years. It was calculated that in the first year £300 would be required for mistresses' salaries, £80 for house rent, and £120 for incidental expenses. In addition to this £500, were the costs of furnishing (including about £1 a head for the necessary school desks, etc.), which he hoped to obtain by way of donation. These figures were accepted by the meeting and a subscription list was to be opened at two local banks. An appeal for funds was to be circulated as widely as possible both in Winchester and throughout Hampshire, together with a prospectus of the proposed school 'so that it may be established with as little delay as possible'.

Miss LeRoy, commenting on the meeting, observed 'it was very helpful to have important men at the first meeting, but unfortunately they knew nothing about Girls' Schools, and that day's success was entirely due to a woman, Miss Westmacott, herself a Headmistress, who though she had never before spoken in public, agreed to come and explain to an ignorant and half-sceptical audience the benefits of a High School education. Those who heard her can never forget how admirably she spoke. She had written out her speech but delivered it by heart, and the men who surrounded her all agreed that no better address could have been made for the occasion'. Miss LeRoy's account continues: 'The next exciting question asked was 'How many names of those wishing to become the first Winchester High School girls would be sent in? And here it may not be uninteresting to reveal a secret. The Council had, in some interval of hopefulness, elected a Headmistress without seeing her, and without having any certain pupils to promise her, or any salary to offer her! This lady, not unnaturally, after a time declined the honour of the Headmistress-ship, and founded an excellent school elsewhere under a more enlightened Council'.

By 14 April 1884 Miss Bramston felt confident enough to write to the *Hampshire Chronicle*:

Winchester High School for Girls

Although I believe that most of those interested in the establishment of the above school have been made acquainted with the following facts it is possible that there are some of your readers who may like to know them: I shall therefore be glad if you will kindly allow me, by means of your paper, to make them public. Somewhat over £800 has been promised, partly in donations, partly in loans; and of this nearly a third has already been paid. This sum, though sufficient to enable the Council to open the school on May 1st, is yet a moderate sum when compared to that usually raised for the starting of a High School, the expenses of which for the first three or four years must necessarily exceed the receipts; promises of further donations or loans will therefore be gladly accepted by the Hon. Treasurer. After very careful consideration of the testimonials of several candidates, the Council have appointed as Head Mistress, Miss Jurgensen of Bedford High School, previously for three years Senior Assistant Mistress at Norwich High School, who holds a Cambridge Higher Local Honour Certificate, had first class distinction in French and German and is L.L.A. of St Andrews (Philology and History) with honours. Her staff, which will consist at first of two trained Assistant Mistresses, will, as the School enlarges, of course be increased. When sufficient promises of pupils from a distance have been sent in, two Boarding Houses, sanctioned by the Council, will be opened; the probable terms of the one of these will be 45 guineas, and those of the other 60 guineas—both inclusive of everything except School Fees.

The fees for day girls were nine, 12 or 15 guineas according to age.

One of the first 17 girls wrote a memoir for the 1934 *Jubilee History*, and she recalled the very first day, 5 May 1884. 'Seventeen girls who I suppose would be called the foundation stones of St Swithun's School [see Appendix One for their names] stood nervously before the Headmistress, Miss Jurgensen, in one of the houses opposite what is now *Southgate Hotel*. They most of them had brothers at school, but none of them had ever been to school themselves or knew in the least what they were expected to do. Miss Jurgensen lived in the house. Her lessons were most inspiring if somewhat alarming at times'.

Another old girl also recalled Miss Jurgensen as an excellent teacher, but possessed of a somewhat volatile temperament and formidable temper. There were three other teachers in the school that first term and the children were divided into three classes. By the second term numbers had grown to about 30, and Miss Wood joined the staff at a salary of £90 a year. She was responsible at first for English, French and Geography, and she observed 'the School was well organised and equipped, but the curriculum was necessarily restricted, neither Science nor German appeared on the timetable'. One of the pupils remembered Miss Wood taking them for drill in the little gravelled back yard which was all they had for recreation. 'One day she backed to give us more room and horrified us by disappearing down a boot-hole in the basement which had never had a grating put over it'.

In April 1885 Miss Jurgensen resigned, and the Council were faced with the necessity of finding a Head Mistress for the next term. They decided to appoint a temporary Head in order to give themselves time to advertise the post, and Miss Mowbray came to fill the gap. When the position was later advertised, she sent in her application with 35 other candidates, and was chosen from them at a starting salary of £200 a year. She had been educated at the North London Collegiate School, and trained at the Home and Colonial Training College. Before coming to Winchester, she had taught at the Liverpool College for Girls and at Clapham High School.

Although all records remain discreetly silent about her age when she was appointed Headmistress, photographs show a slight anxious young woman who cannot have been much more than thirty. With her appointment we can say that the real history of St Swithun's begins. She was to remain Headmistress for 31 years, and all the essential characteristics of St Swithun's today were created by her and her staff, whom by all accounts she chose with great skill. Since she resigned in 1916 there have only been four more Headmistresses, so that the school has a marvellous record of continuity in its leaders which has been one of its great strengths.

There are domestic sciences
for the Lower Vth year

II

Miss Mowbray, 1884-1916

1884-1897

With Miss Mowbray's appointment began a period of steady development which in the next 12 years laid the firm foundations of the school. Its main characteristics were a continuous growth in numbers, demanding first a move into larger premises, and thereafter regular additions to those premises; the establishment of a full teaching staff; the beginnings of boarding houses; the commitment to a high standard of academic excellence and the development of a wide range of extra-curricular activities. These gave so much stimulation and enjoyment to the first generation of girls—dare one say—liberated from the narrowness of their home circle where the range of interests for the average late-Victorian girl was still very limited. The accounts of the school which remain from those early days may seem very naive to us today, but the joy and exhilaration which these girls derived from using their minds and joining in corporate activities demonstrate eloquently the need for such schools. One Old Girl, writing her impressions of the early days of the school, and coming from a small country school where three classes were taught in one big room, said 'I went to Winchester truly mid-Victorian. I had no other experience to shape my expectations but a close study of *Villette* and *Jane Eyre*. I knew no one else who had been to a modern school. Consequently Winchester was a place to me of continual wonder and delight. The glass passage lined with palms and ferns which led to the Hall, the flowers and prints of Old Masters—not wall-maps—in the classrooms surprised me with their beauty. I was delighted by my new surroundings and the general feeling of friendliness which I met everywhere. I had expected to find a bogey among the mistresses; there would be one, I felt sure, who would be severe and unpopular, whose classes would be disliked. I went through my first lessons awaiting anxiously for this bogey. She did not materialize. I was thrilled with Miss Carmichael's English lessons. The word "lessons" is misleading. They were adventures—discoveries. I suppose other people have been as magical in their teaching of English literature, but there were few in those days. History lessons with Miss Mowbray were of sterner stuff—intensely interesting but oh, how stupid I felt, accustomed only to learning by heart facts from the text book, Kings of England, and the battles of the Wars of the Roses. Now I was being asked to consider causes and results, to study characters and movements. I felt completely at sea, and as the quick "Next, next, next" went round the form rapidly approaching me, my heart thumped. Then would come the explanation, vivid and illuminating—a lightning scheme of notes on the board, and the difficult question became comprehensible. Swedish drill with Froken Cederberg was another experience; I had never seen a grown-up in a short tunic before and I much admired the courage with which she stepped out in front of the class regardless of her abbreviated skirts, and the assurance with which she rapped out the bewildering series of commands which everyone else but myself seemed to understand. Science lessons with Miss Martin-Leake were most interesting. Looking back, I can realise even better than I did at the time how well-planned they were, and what splendid training they gave . . . Other conflicts on the hockey field now come to mind. I never got into the 1st eleven but many a game and house match I gasped through on the Wolvesey ground. In those days we wore scarlet tam-o-shanters and dark blue jerseys with the puff sleeves which have come into fashion again this year.'

By January 1886 numbers in the school had grown to over 60. Southgate Street could no longer contain them and so the Council rented a house in St Peter Street from Lord Northbrook. This was to be the School's home for the next 47 years. Although a good deal of it was pulled down to build a cinema after the school sold it, and the garden is now a car park, it is still possible to identify the parts of the building used as the Headquarters of the County Library and for Miss Sprules' Secretarial College: it is difficult to reconcile these remains with Miss Woods' description of it in 1885. 'We were delighted to be transferred to the quiet seclusion of the old house in St Peter Street with its charming lawn belted with trees. There were no omnibuses in those days and little traffic down North Walls. The entrance was then through a conservatory with scarlet geraniums climbing to the roof. The ground floor classes were occasionally distracted by wandering minstrels or an organ grinder and monkey who had gained unauthorised access by the garden gate. Tennis began to be played ...'.

By the time the Annual Meeting was held in June 1885 there were 66 girls in the school. This Annual Meeting was a feature of the school until 1910, when the school was incorporated into a Limited Company, and it took the form of a public meeting at which the Chairman of the Council gave a summary of the year's main events, the annual accounts were presented, and usually a guest speaker was present. These speakers were an impressive collection in the forefront of the educational world, most of them with a particular interest in women's education. In successive years from 1886 they were: Mrs. Bryant, the only woman in England at that time who was both a Doctor of Philosophy and a Doctor of Science; Mrs. Burbury, a governor of North London Collegiate; Mr. W. H. Stone, Chairman of the Girls' Public Day School Company; Miss Emily Davies, one of the most determined fighters of her generation for educational equality for women and the effective founder of Girton College; and Mrs. Wordsworth, the Principal of Lady Margaret Hall.

In 1887 the school invited an outside examiner, a Mr. Tuckwell of the Oxford Local and Oxford and Cambridge Joint Boards, to come to the school, and he reported 'The intellectual tone and vigour of the school are full of promise, the manner and discipline of the girls seem all that could be desired'. This was the prelude to participation in public examinations and the following year five girls took the Cambridge Local Examination which they all passed. By 1893 a regular pattern was established by which girls in the Upper VI took Cambridge Higher Local examinations and those in the Lower VI and V form took the examinations of the Oxford and Cambridge Joint Board. All through these early years Miss Mowbray had been gradually building up an impressively well-qualified staff, and all who knew her speak of her gift for selecting brilliant teachers. Her own teaching, too, earned high praise and in particular she set the tone and standard of the Upper VI. Some charming photographs of her with them during the 1890s survive, headmistress looking not much older than her pupils.

In spite of this dedication to work, and it is interesting to remember that all the regular teaching of the school was confined to the morning between 8.50 and 1.00, the atmosphere of the school was predominantly a family one. 'We really were a family party in those days. No one who joined them will forget the Browning readings we had at Miss Mowbray's house or the country walks she took us, the beginning of nature study'. Another activity entered into school life early on; in 1895 Miss Jameson joined the staff, and as well as introducing the school to hockey, she was one of the pioneers of bicycling for women. She soon got the school, including Miss Mowbray, on to bicycles, and at weekends they went off on picnics into the country and the New Forest; the 'Higher Local Picnic' became an early school tradition to occupy part of the anxious time between the end of the examination and the publication of results. It is clear, too, from the delightful photograph which is reproduced here that the enthusiasm for bicycling was quickly caught by Miss Bramston and Miss LeRoy!

A Games Club was formed in 1894 to provide some sort of substitute exercise for tennis during the winter. During the first winter it was largely the responsibility of the girls; rounders and baseball were played mostly on gravel as the school lawn would not survive such rough use, but it was in danger of foundering until revived in the form of a Hockey Club by Miss Jameson, and, with help from other staff, two XIs were soon got together. The first outside match ever won by the school was in February 1896, against Queen Anne's, Caversham. Miss Jameson is described as wearing a 'trim leather-bound skirt and man-like collar and tie'. The description of the first outside match is worth recording. 'I well remember our first outside match. At that time we had never played on a fast ground, and probably seldom or never with the full number a side. We journeyed by train to play the 2nd XI of a school which prided itself on its efficiency at hockey. We arrived before lunch. Their team were dressed all in scarlet, and looked to us very burly and experienced. The pudding was suet or something of the sort, and was declined by all their players. This impressed us very much. After lunch we were taken round the school buildings and grounds. During this ceremony, according to a story which immediately became current, Miss Morton became separated from her party, and, opening a door by mistake, found the whole of the home team lying down on the floor. Miss Jameson played centre-forward for us, and the Headmistress for them. The Chronicle, I see, draws a discreet veil over the score—I will do likewise—But we did somehow, get one goal.'

All this enthusiasm and activity obviously provoked a strong sense of purpose in the school and the level of achievement was high. In 1893 the first girl went to University, to Lady Margaret Hall, Oxford, and in 1895 the school won its first scholarship: A. Wollaston had been placed first in all England for English Literature in the Cambridge Higher Local Examination and was offered a scholarship at Newnham. Science teaching also began in 1893 and Mabel Clark has left us this description of its early years. 'Miss Fletcher was appointed Science Mistress, and proved a delightfully enthusiastic and interesting teacher. Then began what was for me the most blissful period of School life, for Botany, Geology and Chemistry all became part of our regular life. But we still had no laboratory. Well do I remember these class-room chemistry lessons, when smelly experiments such as the preparation of chlorine had to be hastily pushed outside on the window-sill, and my joy when I was promoted to the honour of cleaning up the mess. I felt I was really advancing and began to cherish dreams of a scholarship and the Natural Sciences Tripos. Apropos of our difficulties, I may mention that when in 1895 the question of a new addition to the building and possibly a laboratory was mooted, the Chemistry class prepared an energetic flask of chlorine mixture and left it where the Visiting Committee could not fail to be conscious of its objectionable odour—whether it influenced their decision or not I do not know, but to our joy we heard the laboratory was to be built.'

'In 1897, four of us entered for our first practical exams. in the Joint Board Certificate. In those days a 'don' was in charge in cap and gown. An enterprising examiner had given red phosphorous as the unknown substance. About ten minutes after we had commenced, a nervous candidate dropped a glowing match on the 'unknown'—result, a wild flare and we all 'knew'. Hardly had the invigilator extinguished this when it was discovered that a pile of dusters was on fire; this in turn was extinguished. Then suddenly the bottom came out of a medicine bottle improvised to contain sodium hydrate, devastating a varnished table and all the candidate's papers. Wearily our friend came for the third time to the rescue, remarking 'my life is insured—I only hope yours are!'. Possibly we had more thrills out of our Science lessons in those days than under modern conditions. To me at least they are a real joy to recall, and to all who taught me I tender my grateful thanks.' What Mabel Clark does not mention in her memoir is that in the same year, 1897, she won the first Science Scholarship for St Swithun's and was one of the seven girls who achieved a University Scholarship that year. The School's academic credentials were triumphantly demonstrated and in fact the achievements of 1897 have never been surpassed.

The same year also saw a very welcome extension of the school's activities. The first *School Chronicle* was printed and it has appeared every year since, except for two years during the 1939-1945 war. We learn from it a good deal about the current school actitivies which had previously only been briefly dealt with in the Annual Report, and in particular another very important school 'first' is recorded. On Saturday 28 November 1896, 12 girls were confirmed by the Bishop in the choir of the Cathedral. This was the first time that a special service had been arranged for the school and the tradition has been unbroken since.

There were already two Societies flourishing in the school, the newly-founded Science Society which has the longest unbroken life of any school society and which boldly stated as its object 'To study nature by actual observations of natural phenomena of all kinds' and a Debating Society which has suffered a number of deaths and resurrections during the life of the school. On this occasion the report begins 'Since the Mistresses have joined this Society the tone of the debates has risen to a distinctly higher level'.

Mission work, which has always been an important element in the school, was evidently already well established, and it is recorded that 'Last year it was decided that our Mission work should in future be carried on in connection with the work of the Women's University Settlement at Southwark. At their suggestion we undertook to do what we could for the children of Belvedere Place Board School, Borough Road.' Money was subscribed termly and used principally in providing for delicate or convalescent children in need of country or sea air. A little boy, Willie Hardy, had been staying with Mrs. Hickman for six weeks at Compton and two little girls were also in the country nearby. Another delightful custom had begun which was to last for a long time, that of sending occasional hampers of flowers during the summer, from Winchester gardens to the London School.

For many years the *School Chronicle* carried a full account of the Old Girls' Association. It was at this time called the W.H.S.O.G.A.—the Winchester High School Old Girls' Association—on which the writer of the Report quite properly comments, 'What a name! Yet we are growing into it. On Thursday June 18th 1896 we celebrated our fifth birthday.' In those days the meeting spread over three days beginning with a 'conversazione' between Old Girls and the present members of the Upper and Lower VI with their own entertainments of music and recitations: on Friday morning Old Girls could attend prayers and lessons (these latter with more enthusiasm than attention, one gathers) and in the afternoon a Tennis Match was played. On this occasion, for the first time, a married Old Girl came with her baby, the School's first 'grandchild'. Tennis was followed by a Literary Meeting where papers were read on books that had been set for reading during the past year and more were chosen for the coming year—three of Robert Louis Stevenson's, *Kidnapped, Memories and Portraits* and *Through the Cevennes on a Donkey*; Matthew Arnold's *Selections*; Miss Benson's *Capital, Labour, Trade and the Outlook*; and Fowle's *The Poor Law*. A business meeting followed after a brief interval for food and the final part of the day's proceedings was a talk on 'Home Life and Economics' by an outside speaker. On Saturday morning there was an 8 o'clock celebration in the Cathedral. One admires the stamina of the participants and the seriousness of purpose, perhaps a little overwhelming to some Old Girls as a note from the Secretary urges them to join the Association and not to be deterred by the literary part of the Society!

One final, interesting, Editorial Note in this first *Chronicle* states that on 5 May 1897 Miss Bramston and Miss LeRoy presented the school with a handsome grandfather clock already more than a hundred years old, on the occasion of its 13th Birthday. That clock now stands in the front hall.

In 1891 the school freed itself of its original debts, the last debenture holder, Mr. Pointer, requesting that the money, £25, be put aside to form the nucleus of a day girl scholarship to enable a girl to go to University. But as soon as the school discharged one set of obligations it acquired another in order to purchase the freehold of the School house and grounds, to build on a large room to serve as a hall, and provide some much needed classrooms and cloakrooms. The Hall was finished in time for the 1891 Annual Meeting which for the first time was held in the School instead of the Guildhall. At that meeting it was reported that for £2,500 the freehold had been bought and extensions completed. During its first 13 years the school had also grown physically in numbers and in buildings and organisation.

After the first abortive attempt to found a boarding house in 1885, High House was established in 1889 in a house rented from Lord Northbrook on St Giles Hill, and is thus the senior of the present houes. It was started by Mrs. Lewis and her friend Miss Tothill with four girls, three seniors and a junior. As was the case with all the boarding houses in the early days, the Housemistress was financially responsible for the house and was answerable to the school only for the well-being of the girls. By 1891 it had its full complement of 15 girls.

In 1892 Mrs. Carbery started a second boarding house in Southgate Street, and after having several different houses she finally settled down in Bereweeke Road in 1895 in a house called Hillcroft: at first this house could only hold eight girls, but it was then enlarged to take 12 to 15 girls. After the First World War they moved again, to St Giles Hill, where the house was able to hold up to 27 girls. Mrs. Carbery and her daughter were both very musical and started the first school orchestra, although from the very beginning music was an important part of school life. It was one of Miss Mowbray's great interests and her sister, Miss Esther Mowbray, was a member of the music staff for many years.

A third house, the Homestead, was also established in 1892, in Bereweeke Road. It survived for only seven years, but its only housemistress, Miss Craig, wrote a vivid account of its short life for the 1934 *History* and in describing the social work of the house said 'one summer, early on Saturday mornings, two girls would take flowers for the prisoners' breakfast table at Fulflood Schools. On that day each week, prisoners were discharged from the County Gaol and met and fed by a Parochial Committee'. She also remembered the house helping to clothe a 'very poor child from Wales Street who used to come up periodically to be measured for flannel petticoats and other garments'.

By 1895 the school had grown to over 100, and more building became necessary. A large new block was added in 1896 bringing the school buildings up to the very edge of North Walls: a contributor to the first *Chronicle*, while admitting its necessity, says 'Outwardly [its] appearance is not prepossessing—a block of red brick, red-tiled buildings, perfectly flat with rows of windows, rises abruptly from the pavement of North Walls to a height of three stories in the middle and two at each side; the ends of the gables being painted green the effect is not unlike that of the traditional Noah's Ark.' As this part of the original buildings has survived, the present generation can pass its own judgement, but certainly the general aspect from North Walls is pretty bleak. However, it contained the first proper laboratory and a dining room, as well as new music rooms and class rooms.

It also provided house rooms for the two newly-formed day-girl houses—Town houses they were called at first. Miss Finlay, in the 1934 *History*, explained that with the establishment of the boarding houses, the day girls, numbering about half the school, began to find themselves in an anomalous position. 'They seemed so unshepherded, apart from their Form life, while the esprit de corps of each boarding house grew and strengthened. The need for some fresh organisation was evident, and the system of Town houses, which had worked so well at Clifton College, was suggested and tried ... the eventful afternoon arrived when the scheme ... was to be put before (the girls). Those whose name began with the letters A to G, the future Caer Gwent, were summoned to the dining room, those to be in Venta, H to Z, met in the room above, probably at that date the Upper VI. Rumours were rife, excitement ran high, and here an eye-witness, the only one of both these epoch-making meetings, had a good story to tell!

"Miss Martin-Leake, our lately arrived Science Mistress, presided as House Mistress over Caer Gwent in the dining room, with her helper (and successor) Miss Billson. Above, with the budding Venta, was Miss Jameson, Senior Mathematical Mistress and now House Mistress, with Miss Arthur, who had newly joined the music staff, as her colleague. Downstairs, all was orderly, everyone most interested, paying proper attention to what Miss Martin-Leake had to say, not, indeed, asking many questions, or venturing opinions, but pondering over the whole matter. Upstairs, happy pandemonium! One from Caer Gwent had to to up, either to ask a question and or give information, more probably the latter, and the impression gathered was that everyone was talking at once, voices growing louder and louder, Miss Jameson ringing the only bell the School possessed, Miss Arthur looking on in quiet and amused astonishment. It was evident, however, that everyone was enjoying the whole proceeding immensely. And so," says Eye-witness, "that is how the Town Houses began." '

The plight of the day girls had been accentuated by the formation of a fourth Boarding House in the spring of 1896. This was Earlsdown, on St Giles Hill, started by Miss M. du Boulay. There were 10 girls to begin with, mostly already known to her, which made, as she said, 'a sort of pleasant family party with practically no rules beyond the ordinary courtesies of life'. The chief problem was 'the long daily trudge to School down the hill and up again, and for games down the hill to Wolvesey and up again and the girls were often very tired. There were no motor cars or 'buses available in those days so we started with a donkey cart to carry the bags, and later on changed to a pony and trap but even so only one or possibly two girls could be sure of a lift.'

At the Annual Meeting of 1897, the Chairman reported that the sanatorium for the boarding houses had been built 'on a high and breezy down'. Thus Winchester High School for Girls made its first contact with the future home of St Swithun's, for the building just then completed still stands in a corner of the Playing Fields, and indeed, the school in 1897 is already recognisable as the St Swithun's of today with its academic success, a special connection with the Cathedral, concern for others' welfare and, more tangibly, the establishment of three of the five existing boarding houses and the two day houses.

1897-1909

While it might be true to say that the school showed little apparent sign of change between 1897 and when it came to celebrate its quarter-century in 1909, this is not to imply that it had simply stood still in the intervening 12 years. On the contrary, they were ones of steady growth, springing from the roots so firmly planted in the first 13 years of its existence.

When the Dean, as Chairman, gave his Annual Report at the end of 1897, he was able to include in his speech the names of seven girls who had won scholarships to University in that year. He probably felt, too, that this was a suitable occasion to point out that the scholarship fund, so generously started with the money from the last of the original debentures in 1890, had not made any great progress. It had grown from £25 to £80 only, and he felt that 'it would be a very happy recognition of the good work done in the school' if parents made some small contribution to the fund. It was after this that the suggestion was made that such a fund should be linked with the name of Charlotte Yonge as a memorial to her life-work; Miss LeRoy, fittingly perhaps, as she was also a prolific and successful author of historical novels under the name of Esme Stuart, became the secretary of the fund raising efforts and the most energetic worker for the cause. At the Annual Meeting in December 1899 it was announced that the fund now amounted to £2,030 and that the Trust Deed for the scholarship had just been signed. One clause of the deed stated ' ... a fund has recently been raised by subscriptions received from various people in England and many other parts of the world in honour of the said Charlotte Mary Yonge for the part she has taken during the last sixty years in the advancement of religious education by means of her published literary works, which fund ... is intended to be applied towards assisting girls who are or have been educated in the said High School to obtain the advantages of attendance at the Universities of Oxford or Cambridge or some other University situated in the United Kingdom or Ireland'. To a particularly large audience gathered to hear the announcement of the inauguration the Dean went on to list the conditions of the scholarship which was to be awarded by examination once every two years and to have a value of not less than £40 annually. The first election would be made in 1900.

The first Charlotte Yonge Scholar was Amy Locke, who won an open scholarship to Somerville where she read History. She proved to be a more than worthy recipient of the award—she became a professional historian working for most of her short life on the Victoria County History where her work was highly praised. Unfortunately her health broke down and she died prematurely in June 1916. Fittingly she was buried close to Miss Yonge's grave in Otterbourne churchyard.

The school had its own celebration for the inauguration of the Scholarship: in the summer a party was held and a presentation made by the Bishop of Winchester to Miss Yonge of an illuminated address (which was later given back to the school by Miss Yonge's family and now hangs in the Waiting Room) and a book containing the names of all the subscribers to the fund. In her biography of Charlotte Yonge (Constable, 1943), Georgina Battiscombe describes the event. 'Charlotte's behaviour at public functions was always a source of anxiety to those responsible for the success of the occasion for the chilliness of her manner could be enough to damp the most enthusiastic gathering, but even the formidable barrier of her shyness melted a little before the warmth of the welcome that greeted her appearance in the School Hall, appropriately decorated for the occasion with heartsease and daisies. Escorted by Bishop Randall Davidson and followed by Aimé LeRoy and Anna Bramston, two of the most faithful of her one-time Goslings, she passed between the rows of excited school girls, a tall, erect figure, dressed in black mantle and plain black bonnet in startling contrast to her fair complexión and abundant masses of snow-white hair. From her seat of honour on the platform Charlotte listened to the future Archbishop of Canterbury proclaiming his childhood's love for *The Little Duke* and declaring "I for one thank God I am here today to bear testimony, and to take part in a presentation which comes from loyal hearts to one whom we desire to revere". Every one of her admirers, from the Princess of Wales down to the smallest schoolgirl present, seemed to have joined together to do her honour. The words of the illuminated address presented to her stressed the world-wide nature of her influence and appeal: "From all parts of England and Wales, from Scotland and Ireland, contributions have been sent, so that this scholarship has become the embodiment of the love, admiration, and gratitude which the donors feel for you. From scattered homes in Canada and South Africa, from New Zealand and India, from Australia, the Falkland Islands, and Buenos Aires, as well as from the United States of America, has come the echo of the deep sense of the obligation we owe to you and their wish to share with us the pleasure of being able to express it during your lifetime".

Charlotte had reached her apotheosis. Yet even now as an old and famous woman she was the same bashful, self-conscious creature that she had been as a girl of seventeen. As she rose to reply her hands shook visibly and her admirably-phrased expressions of pleasure and gratitude were delivered in a curiously high-pitched voice that quavered with nervousness. A schoolgirl performance of tableaux scenes chosen from her historical stories and ending with a 'daisy chain' dance restored her equanimity.'

Physically and in numbers the school grew in the early years of the century: in 1900 and 1902 further additions to the buildings were made and thereafter its appearance did not alter greatly during the rest of the school's life in North Walls. By the turn of the century numbers had grown to 170 with 15 other girls coming in for occasional classes (they were known at first by the rather unfortunate title of 'outsiders', later as 'by-students') and in 1902 after the closing of the Homestead, another boarding house, Hyde Abbey, much nearer the main school building, was opened by Mrs.

Towers Thompson. It was an old house which had been a boys' school of some importance in the 18th century, and Benjamin Disraeli had received some of his education there.

The next real development was a project obviously very dear to Miss Mowbray: she had not been well at the beginning of 1902 and had a sabbatical term that autumn. This perhaps gave her both time to think, and renewed energy to carry through a very bold and possibly over-ambitious scheme which came to be known as the 'New School'. Miss Mowbray herself said at the Old Girls' Association Meeting in 1904 'It is a development of an old idea. A few of you can well remember the difficulty of dealing with the girl who came at fourteen and left at sixteen, a twelve years' course to be got through in two years. In our New School we lay ourselves out to meet this difficulty.' Specifically, it was designed to provide a more suitable education for the girl who would leave school at 15 or 16 rather than at 18 or 19 as was more common then, and its fees were to be very modest. It was housed in No. 14 St Peter Street and opened in September 1903 with 21 pupils; by November 1904 it had 36 pupils. This was the highest total of pupils, and it must remain a matter of speculation as to why it did not grow as fast as its parent school had done, especially as it had many of the same teachers and the use of all the facilities of the High School just across the street. Possibly the demand for secondary education for girls in Winchester had been satisfied, possibly there was not the same social cachet in having a daughter at the 'New' School. One cannot tell what would have happened if it had continued, but by 1906 the County Authority had decided to open a school of its own in the town which was intended to serve almost exactly the same purpose as the 'New' School, and the Council of the High School took the decision to close their venture rather than engage in any competition.

Miss Mowbray spoke of her disappointment to the Old Girls, but another innovation on which she embarked at the same time was to prove much more fruitful and rewarding. This was the establishment of a course for training teachers within the school. Before it could be set up the school had to be inspected by the Board of Education to see whether it was suitable for training teachers for registration: a report was received by the Council approving the scheme and saying 'This is an excellent school, doing most useful work. Great care and attention is given, not only to intellectual work, but to the general welfare of the girls. There are ample opportunities for physical exercise and other occupations.' Thereafter, until 1919, the school always had some teachers in training. At the other end of the age-range, the school was extended to include a Kindergarten which for a long period took boys of pre-prep school age as well as girls.

Other extensions of school activity took place, and the school's involvement with the town was certainly increased during the period of the Cathedral restoration in the early years of the century. In 1906 the school held a great sale of household linen made by members of the school and contributed by them, their parents and friends, and by Old Girls. Entertainments were also provided by the school, including *Living Statues* and a French play, both of which proved so popular that repeat performances had to be given. The sum of £181 was realised, a very large amount of money for those days, and paid for several thousand bags of cement with which the Cathedral sub-structure was being reinforced. Afterwards a tour of the Cathedral was arranged for some of the senior girls. They saw the famous diver, William Walker, who was responsible for clearing much of the peat on which it was found that the Cathedral foundation rested, and putting in its place thousands of bags of cement. They were able to look down the great hole made outside the north wall of the Cathedral from which passages were dug under the Cathedral itself. The passages themselves were full of peaty water and the diver was working in the dark by feel alone, laying 60 to 70 blocks of cement in his hour-and-a-half stints. While the girls were there the diver came up and they were able to talk to him and look at his equipment. In this they were greatly honoured, as they were the first unofficial visitors to see the work in progress.

But, for the school, as for Winchester itself , the high point of the fund-raising efforts was the famous pageant of 1908 which took place in the grounds of Wolvesey Palace depicting 1200 years of the city's history. The school, in a sense, was doubly involved, as Miss LeRoy contributed much to the script and the school performed a flower dance during the last episode of Charles II's visit to Winchester. Dressed as different flowers, 116 girls took part, and the editor of the *Chronicle* recorded 'Even school work was set aside for the all-important Pageant, and we are glad to feel that this unusual concession was justified by the result for there is no doubt that our dance was universally appreciated. The Princess Louise thanked us personally . . .'. *The Times* reported 'A charming incident was the dance of 116 girls from the Winchester High School in which the exquisite colouring of the simple dresses and the beauty of the figures were beyond praise' and the *Daily Mail* spoke of 'A dance . . . which, for delicate graduations and combinations of colour, and for joyous grace of movement, it would be impossible to beat'. A rather faint photograph of the Earlsdown girls in their pageant dresses shows them in long pale full garments with stronger coloured scarves, their hair loose and with wreaths of flowers on their heads. A member of High House remembered being escorted up and down St Giles Hill for rehearsals in full costume by her housemistress, Mrs Thomas, who was dressed as a medieval peasant.

Apart from this participation in the Pageant, members of the school were beginning to go to concerts in the town and to the Greek play at Bradfield, but most of their cultural and extra-curricular activities still took place in the school. Music was a very strong interest with chamber recitals being given by members of the music staff and in 1906 a Glee Club was started. Acting, too, had always been a part of the school's life and innumerable performances were put on, usually at house level: episodes from History seem to have been very popular, also tableaux. Lectures tended to be serious and instructive. In 1908, for instance, two courses of University Extension lectures were given in the school on Carlyle and Ruskin. There were talks on 'An English Public School in Syria', Hexham Abbey, 'Some Phases of Medieval Life in Hampshire', Piers Plowman and 'The Sweating System in connection with some English Industries'. The school joined the League of Empire in 1905 and was affiliated to the Advanced School in Adelaide and a school in Maritzburg in South Africa. This led to visits from staff from overseas and correspondence with other affiliated schools.

There was also the Mission work. This was something about which Miss Mowbray felt very strongly, and more than once in her addresses at Old Girls' Meetings she expressed a wish that Old Girls should take up mission work in England in the Settlements, or abroad. In 1903 the mission work which the school had been supporting in Borough Road came to a natural end, and the school joined the U.G.S.M. which worked mainly in Camberwell and Peckham and supported a mission house in Peckham Road. Both present members of the school and Old Girls were organised to give support, and Old Girls in particular were encouraged to spend some time in the mission house to help with the regular work. Parties of girls used to go up each year to the U.S.G.M. Annual Thanksgiving Service in Southwark Cathedral, and often visited the Settlement in St Mark's Parish which was their special interest. One such visit was reported by one of the girls. 'Outside the Boys' Club had congregated another crowd of pale, eager children. Shyness was wearing off and we were able to find several of our own "children" among them. In our enthusiasm we all too hastily enquired if there were any who had not got a "lady" and would like to be written to. This was to fire a train of gunpowder. Immediately each of us was surrounded by a host of little creatures, begging, but not a bit roughly or rudely, to be written to.'

In 1909, through the U.M.C.A., a small African boy named Albano was 'adopted' by the school and this began a long association with African children being educated at a mission school at Magila in Zanzibar, some of whom were more successful than others. A member of staff at the High School co-ordinated the school's efforts and for a long time Albano persisted in writing to 'Miss Little's children'. Albano's successor, Mliangu, was so spoilt and disobedient that the mission school had to expel him for a time, and his successor, Lucy, evidently married rather precipitately before she had finished her education.

By 1900 both tennis and hockey were firmly established as school games and regular matches were played against the Godolphin School in Salisbury as well as occasional hockey matches against teams from the Oxford women's colleges. Then in 1905 lacrosse was introduced. In all games the coaches were members of the ordinary teaching staff and the prosperity of any one game depended very much on the enthusiasm of the particular staff of the moment. Lacrosse, for instance, was nearly still-born, for the only member of staff with a real knowledge of the game left after a week, but then another member of staff came to the rescue though her own knowledge of the game was very limited. The first real boost to interest in the game was given when, in 1907, arrangements were made for 24 girls to visit Wycombe Abbey who had been playing for some years. They started out at 9 a.m. and arrived back at 8 p.m., were given lunch in the houses at Wycombe and took part in a game and were given some coaching. In the same season the school team played its first outside matches, one against Queen Anne's, Caversham, thereafter to be its fiercest rival, and the other against Godolphin, also to become an annual and strongly-fought fixture.

The Old Girls' Association continued to hold its three-day meetings, and from 1903 onwards the *Chronicle* carried an annual account of Old Girls' work, which contains much interesting information for the school itself, and also is of value as social history. Most years the *Chronicle* included two or three letters from Old Girls which were considered of particular interest. For 1903 the record shows that there were three headmistresses and two others teaching abroad and in England 19 Old Girls had teaching posts in schools, amongst them three at the High School itself, others at Roedean, the Royal School, Bath, and Bedford College, and there were others in private teaching. Six girls were nursing and amongst other occupations in the list are Art school training, book-binding, photography, missionary and social work. Professional gardening became popular too.

Amongst the earliest letters written to the *Chronicle* are two accounts of University life, one from Royal Holloway and one from St Hugh's, Oxford. These were, perhaps, prompted by authority to encourage other girls to attempt University Entrance. The letters give a picture of days divided pleasurably between work and sport, and in both cases ending with cocoa parties or 'the coa-coa' as the undergraduate at St Hugh's puts it: her comment is 'At 10 o'clock these dismal things called coa-coas begin, and I may here add that the formal coa-coa to which the Senior invites the Fresher, and the Fresher the Senior, is the most harrowing function that ever woman student instituted'.

A rather livelier existence is described by Violet Hart (who, as Violet Polunin, painted Miss Mowbray's portrait) in the life of an art student in Paris, although it appears that the girls were segregated in the teaching studios. Her description reads like that of a stage set for La Boheme: 'Those who come to Paris merely as visitors know but little of the Latin quarter and its inhabitants. Before I came to this quarter I thought of Paris as a place where people dressed well and amused themselves. That side of Parisian life is to be found in the Bois de Boulogne and the Champs Elysees, where the gaily dressed ladies certainly appear to have nothing better to think about than their poodles, their costumes and other people's opinion of them. In the Latin quarter it is quite different. Everyone is studying or working in some way. The streets literally swarm with students of every description and almost every nationality. There are medical students who are always noted for their rowdiness, although I do not know how they can be more wild than art students if all the stories one hears of the latter be true. There are students from the Sorbonne and other colleges, their black portfolios bulging with books under their arms, rummaging in the second-hand book stalls along the quays. There are art students, truly weird objects, with their ancient jerseys and coats, their enormous, baggy corduroy trousers fastened round the ankle, their soft felt hats battered into some strange form, and their long hair falling on to their shoulders. A new comer when he first joins their ranks has rather a hard time. To begin with he has to "treat" all his fellow students, of whom there may be thirty or more. Then he is given a warm welcome, or, to speak more plainly, he is half roasted. He is tied to an easel, paraffin is poured on the floor in a circle around him and lighted. Another form of welcoming a stranger is to light a heap of brown paper under his stool and let it smoulder, half choking him. Sometimes a bonfire of chairs and easels is made in his honour.'

Quite another way of life is described by another Old Girl, Annie Turner, who was keeping house for her two brothers farming in the Transvaal. 'You must not think we are living in a Park Lane mansion, furnished throughout by Maple, for we live in a house where nearly all the furniture is home-made by the boys themselves, and our walls of mud are just washed over with pink wash. Our ceilings are of calico, being cheaper than boarding; and our dining room floor is of crushed ant heap. My wardrobe is made from an old chicken hutch, and our small tables and washing stands of boxes turned up on end. Our utensils too are primitive. An old cigarette tin pierced with holes is a grate; old lard tins cut down, our baking tins; an old broken down tin meat safe, a dressing table (this is hardly a utensil though), an old bottle our rolling pin and a piece of newspaper on our one tray, our pastry board. I object to the former as the print is apt to come off on the pastry, but the boys do not mind.

We do our own butchering amongst other things, and I find that one soon gets used to cutting up an ox or a sheep, and having a sheep or fowl killed just outside the door! I am getting quite an adept at driving a pair of mules across the veldt and quite enjoy chasing cows, calves, or pigs when required.'

One last event must be recorded in this section since it brought the High School significantly nearer its present home. After the 1908 Pageant, the ground at Wolvesey which had been the school's main playing field was apparently no longer available—possibly the Pageant had been altogether too much for it—and for a season the school had to divide for games, some playing on a field near Earlsdown, and some near Hillcroft. Then a site of 10 acres became available on Morn Hill, which the Council rented at the end of 1908, and this ground is still part of the present playing fields. The Annual Report for 1909 pointed out that the girls had the advantage of beautiful views and beautiful air. This was indeed so, but generations of school girls who were not fortunate enough to live in Earlsdown or the High House remember the long trek up and down from the town carrying all their equipment.

1909-1916

The years 1909 and 1910 were both years of celebration. In 1909 the school celebrated its 25th anniversary, and in the following year Miss Mowbray completed 25 years as Headmistress. Whether or not it was in anticipation of these two events the school invested in a Union Jack, a flag of St George, and a flagstaff 36 feet high! Other events worthy of record in that year include the first use of the new playing fields, the substitution of lacrosse for hockey as the main winter game and the appearance on the staff, for 18 months only, of the school's first games coach, Miss Gibson. During the year the whole school was examined in the art of setting gathers into a band and in putting a sleeve into a nightgown, and a new two-year course in domestic science and housecraft was to be introduced for a special class of girls in the senior school who were not going to remain long enough to get into the VI form. Numbers remained much as they had been at the beginning of the century: in 1909 there were 172 girls in the school with 20 'outsiders', and, on average, five girls a year were going on to University.

There seems to have been no special celebration for the school's quarter-centenary; the rejoicings and congratulations were saved up for the following year when it was Miss Mowbray's turn. And quite rightly; she and Miss Bramston were the real creators of the school and literally gave their whole lives to it in a way which it is difficult to imagine today. The main celebrations took place during the Old Girls' weekend, when Miss Mowbray was presented with gifts; a bertha of Point-de-gâze lace, a Chesterfield sofa and a silver tea service and spirit kettle. She in her turn gave to the school a cast of Michelangelo's plaque of the Holy Family, thus adding to the already formidable collection of reproductions of works of art, mainly of the Renaissance period, which seem to have been the almost obligatory choice of anyone wishing to make a present to the school at that time. At the celebration lunch there were 118 Old Girls present, and it was reported 'The Hall seemed quite full, and complaints even reached our ears, that owing to the prevailing fashion in hats, some had to take turns to eat their luncheon'. A photograph taken during the weekend shows very clearly 'the prevailing fashion in hats'. In her speech of thanks, Miss Mowbray recalled the very beginning of her association with the school. 'I am getting old enough to love to recall the past, and every detail of Easter Tuesday, 1885, is still a vivid memory—my getting a letter to say a temporary Head Mistress was wanted here—my reading out with much amusement the suggestion that I should apply—the taking the letter to my mother's room, and to my own surprise, as much as her's, finding myself saying "I am going down to Winchester, mother". On arriving I was directed to Culver's Close, only to hear that Miss Bramston was "not at home". On the way back to the station I called in the School for a Prospectus, and found I should have asked for Miss A. R. Bramston, so at last I arrived at Witham Close, and found the Committee Meeting for the appointment of Head Mistress just separating, having decided that none of the applicants would do. Miss Moberly, Miss Bramston, and Miss LeRoy were still there, and I had a delightful talk before my train to town, a very little about schools, and much about a new volume of Browning's poems just out, and which I had with me. Then there were the first few weeks, April and May, full of the sunshine of spring—weeks in which I became so devoted to the School and Winchester that it would hve been a great grief if the Council had not offered me the post on that 27th May.' One sadness was that Miss Bramston could not be there to share the occasion with them, but she had been ill and for the first time had had to miss an Old Girls' Meeting.

Another sadness that the school must have suffered at this time was in connection with Captain Scott's Antarctic Expedition. They had enthusiastically collected money to provide equipment for the expedition: it had been hoped to provide a sledge and when that proved too expensive, a dog. One house was concerned, however, about the ultimate fate of the dog, but they need not have worried as in the postscript to a formal letter acknowledging the gift of money, Captain Scott wrote in his hand 'Will you please give my hearty thanks to the girls for their subscription and good wishes. I'm sorry to say that all the dogs have been named already, but I will devote your donation to the purchase of a tent which will be called "Winton" and will help to keep us warm!—R.S.' Alas, not warm enough!

The four years that yet remained before the First World War were ones of change for the School, particularly in matters of organisation. In 1910 a major change of status in the school took place; it became an Incorporated Company and the Association of the Winchester High School for Girls was formed. As the Dean explained at the last Annual Public Meeting at which, incidentally, an Old Girl of the school, Muriel Stratton, was present in her capacity as Mayoress of Winchester, 'the main object in doing this was simply to facilitate business matters'. It made no difference to the Constitution of the Council, but in future the accounts would be passed by the Council, and the election of new members of the Council would be undertaken by the Council itself. Invitations were sent out to supporters of the school inviting them to become members of the Association, and of the 40 circulated, 19 accepted and became its first members.

As a result of this change in status, the method of keeping the school records changed, and from this date onwards an unbroken series of minutes of Council meetings exists. For many years, also, the Headmistress's reports to the meetings survive, and the picture of the day to day events in the school becomes more detailed and interesting as a result.

It is clear from the minutes of the first Council Meeting, that scholarships to the Boarding Houses were already in existence, and by 1912 a Scholarship for an Overseas Student had been added, largely due to the initiative of Miss Mowbray who had been in correspondence with overseas headmistresses. Through this she had discovered that girls who were capable of going on to higher education were often unable to do so as their parents could not finance the cost of sending them to England and maintaining them there. They were to be selected by nomination rather than examination, and it was felt better that they should come into the school in the summer rather than the autumn as the weather would be more suitable for those coming from hot climates.

The first Overseas Scholar, Constance Wimble, nominated by Miss du Boulay in the Transvaal, arrived in 1912, and she was followed in 1913 by two more, one from India, and Marjorie Hallett, nominated by Miss Gosling in Bermuda, and who returned to Bermuda to become headmistress of her old school, the Bermuda High School. Apparently when Miss Gosling told Marjorie that she was going to Winchester the child 'gasped and then blurted out "it is what I have dreamt of all my life".' Miss Gosling added in her letter 'It means more than I can tell you to this small but ancient colony where we have always prided ourselves on our loyalty but where there is great danger of overmuch American influence'. Overseas Scholars continued to come at intervals up to the Second World War. The majority of them were of British nationality, but one girl came from Egypt on the nomination of her government in 1925. As she was a Moslem it was thought desirable that she should lodge in the town, rather than living in the school. This seems to have been the normal practice with girls of other religions at this time, as there are records of two Hindus and a Jewess all being similarly accommodated in the 1920s.

The other matter which occupied a good deal of time in Council meetings during 1912 and 1913 was the possibility of changing the name of the school. The matter seems to have had its genesis in a letter signed by the Housemistresses written to Miss Bramston in 1912. Evidently this was not the first time they had written, as they say 'We are writing to urge you once again to bring before the Council the imperative need we feel that the school should no longer be called a "High School". It has been brought home to us again and again since we last wrote, that we are losing girls for no other reason than that the school is called a High School and consequently now-a-days confused with the County Schools and parents refuse to come and interview us on that account when friends tell them of the School and urge them to send their children there·. . . we are essentially of the Public Schools type and ought not to lay ourselves open to be confused with the County Schools . . .'. Their suggestion was that the word 'High' be dropped from the school's title and that it become 'The Winchester School for Girls' but when the matter came before the Council for discussion a positive shower of other suggestions descended. 'St Swithun's School for Girls', 'St Mary's', and 'King Alfred's' were the most popular, and at that first meeting 'St Mary's' (although at first vote 'St Swithun's' had the most support), carried the day. But second, and indeed third, thoughts were had before the original suggestion of the Housemistresses—'The Winchester School for Girls'—was accepted as the most satisfactory solution, and after all the formalities had been completed, in 1914, the school underwent its first change in name. It is clear, however, that this was never regarded as wholly satisfactory, as at intervals until 1927, when the name was finally changed to 'St Swithun's', rumblings were heard from such various sources as Old Girls, Staff and the Council themselves.

In 1913 the school had its first fully-documented inspection by the Board of Education, and from its report much of interest emerges on every conceivable aspect of the school's life. For instance 'Class of life from which pupils are drawn' was expressed in percentages: Professional, 60 per cent; Farmers, 7 per cent; Wholesale traders, 11 per cent; Retail traders, 17 per cent; Clerks and Commercial agents, 1 per cent; Public Service, 2 per cent; Occupation unclassified, 2 per cent: and so was 'Areas from which pupils are drawn': Winchester, 46 per cent; Rest of Hampshire, 18 per cent; Rest of England, 24 per cent; Places outside England, 12 per cent.

The numbers in the school had shown a downward trend over the last five years, from 175 to 145 (and indeed there had been some concern in the Council about this), and the total number of staff employed was 26, of which 11 were full time.

Fees showed astonishingly little increase in 29 years. Tuition fees for Day Girls ranged from approximately £8 to £20 for the year, with boarders paying slightly more, and yearly boarding fees varied between £42 and £84, so £108 was the most that could be paid for any girl in one year.

As is usual in these reports, sanitary arrangements got a great deal of attention, and were thought to be somewhat below standard requirements, but it is clear that in the boarding houses each girl had her own self-contained cubicle and washing arrangements, and garden and playground space was thought to be generous. The school food came in for praise with lunch costing 10d a day on a regular basis.

Much of the report is properly taken up with the academic work, and there is little real criticism. Almost all the girls did at least one year's Latin, taught in its early stages mainly by oral and conversational methods, but rather less than half continued with it; Greek was taught from the Upper V onwards and at that time there were, altogether, about 15 girls learning it. It was commented that the amount of time in the week given to classical languages was very short, and since almost all the girls took German as well as French, it might be better educationally to offer Latin and German as alternatives at first although this would be more expensive in staff. In Science, the teaching was thought to be good, and the enthusiasm for the subject beyond what is usually found in a girls' school. The Mathematics teaching came in for high praise, particularly that of the Senior Mistress (who was the recently-appointed Dorothy Clark, an Old Girl of the school), who was judged to be an inspiring teacher of her subject, and the attention and brightness of the classes in her hands suggested no ordinary skill. She showed promise of being a brilliant teacher, a prediction her subsequent career amply justified. Music, too, was regarded as being an important factor in the life of the school 'which is to be congratulated on possessing a very able staff'.

For Miss Mowbray there was the highest and warmest praise as being absolutely devoted and ungrudging of her time, and she is commended to the Governing Body as deserving very well of them indeed. The general conclusion was that the organisation and discipline of the school were entirely satisfactory with a high tone and standard of life, the girls responding easily and readily to the excellent influences of those in authority.

One thing which the Report did not mention in detail was the type of games played, and it is, perhaps, worth recording that in 1912 cricket was added to tennis as a summer game.

In August 1914 the First World War began, and some girls were unable to return to school in the Autumn term because they—temporarily—could not leave France, or because fathers had joined up and the family had moved, but other than an almost complete cessation of lectures and concerts the first major impact of the War on the school (one does not know about early casualties among the families of girls and staff) came on 3 January 1915, during the holdiays, when Mr. and Mrs. White, the school caretakers, were told that the school was to be requisitioned and to expect 400 troops within the hour. These troops were from the Royal Fusiliers and the East Surrey Regiment. The reason for this was that owing to an incessant downpour of rain in the New Year the army camps on Magdalen Hill had to be evacuated and any empty buildings were taken over to house them. The 'occupation' lasted until 19 January, during which time horses were picketed on the lawn and waggons and watercarts drawn up there, while the main school entrance was guarded by a sentry with a fixed bayonet.

Term was due to begin only two days after the troops left, and the state of the school was 'discouraging', so the beginning of term was postponed for another four days. Even though a 'small army of charwomen' descended, followed by decorators, the main building was not yet fit for use, and for the first fortnight of term the teaching was done in the boarding houses and in rooms kindly lent by townspeople. Miss Mowbray described how the time-table was rearranged and 'worked without a hitch even though staff were moving from house to house and even from town to hill'. She added (perhaps prophetically) 'Many of us were, I know, sorry to leave the wonderful air of the hill even for our more commodious building. On our return the change in the school was indeed wonderful. Miss Dennett and I had worked in the school immediately after the soldiers left and it seemed impossible that it could ever be clean and fresh again. The impossible had, however, become possible.' The worst casualty was the lawn, which had to be returfed, and it emerged from discussion (over the amount of compensation due) with the officer in command that the occupation had been a mistake 'done suddenly and without sufficient thought' and that he felt that he should personally bear the expense of repair, which he duly did! This incident must have added considerably to the pressure on Miss Mowbray who had already had a sabbatical term in the summer of 1911 for the sake of her health, and she was ill again for the first half of the Summer term of 1915. The strains of war were ever-present in Winchester as it was a garrison town and a staging post for troops embarking from Southampton and Portsmouth for France. One Old Girl's memory of school during the war is of endless long columns of marching men and the difficulty of crossing the road between them when going down and up St Giles Hill. The troops brought illness with them into the town and at intervals during the war anxiety about the girls going out into the town was expressed in Council meetings. Food prices rose sharply and the housemistresses asked whether it would be possible to increase boarding fees; they suggested alternatively that the length of terms should be cut to save expense. Mrs. Thomas at High House was an early casualty: her health gave out in the summer of 1915 and her resignation led to the first steps in the process of making the school wholly responsible for the running and financing of the boarding houses. At a Council meeting at which the housemistresses were present in July 1915, uniform fees for the Boarding Houses were agreed, and a suggestion was made that they should in future be collected by the school, but this was not acceptable to the older generation of Housemistresses who preferred to keep their independence. It was noted, however, that this might be possible in the future, and the Council took a hand in the negotiations transferring the lease of High House from Mrs. Thomas to Miss Fisher, making itself responsible for the purchase of furniture and the payment of delapidations.

In the end, Miss Mowbray's health broke down irretrievably in February 1916, and she was advised that she should give up her work at the end of that term. Once again, as when she was appointed, the Council was faced with the necessity of finding a successor in haste, but in every other respect the contrast could not have been greater. She was leaving a school secure and successful and nationally recognised as one of the leading girls' schools—so much so that when the Prussian Government had sent one of its Privy Councillors to observe English education in 1911 he was advised by the Board of Education to pay a visit to the Winchester High School for Girls. That this was due to her inspiration cannot be doubted, and it is only sad that we are now largely dependent on written reminiscences and photographs to try and build up a picture of her. But one of her Old Girls, Phyllis Wincott (1908-1909) spoke recently of her most warmly, saying that once known she was never forgotten, in appearance tall, slim with a pale complexion and grey blue eyes, not fashionable in her dress and always wearing a high boned collar, popular with the girls as always being just and kind. Miss Wincott remembered being summoned to her study just before her confirmation and being given a prayer-book in which Miss Mowbray had written— (Miss Wincott having, she said, deservedly, a reputation for being lazy)—'Whatever your hand findeth to do, do it with all your MIGHT'. This appropriate and astringent comment accords well with another recorded piece of advice to girls nervous of performing in public at one of the school concerts 'Children, don't let your teeth chatter, but if they must, don't let the world hear them'. One of the school's most distinguished Old Girls, Enid Locket (nee Rosser) sent to the school the relevant part of a memoir she had written for a grand-daughter shortly before she died in 1980. She went to school in 1916 and knew Miss Mowbray for two terms: writing of her retirement and the arrival of her successor, Miss Finlay, Mrs. Locket says 'At the end of my second term Miss Mowbray retired to be replaced as Headmistress by Miss Finlay. Miss Finlay could not have been more different than Miss Mowbray. She had lovely red hair, was as gentle as Miss Mowbray was fierce. She was elegant with a soft voice . . . She was very much younger of course and of the new generation of school mistresses. She lacked the tremendous authority which those older women possessed and I personally am glad that I knew these old magnificent women even though they could strike terror into the hearts of the young. They inspired with their grand integrity and their belief that women had a right to the independent lives. It is difficult to explain their influence. Their standards of behaviour were high and they were uncompromising in their beliefs. We laughed at them and they caused us much heart burning, but they passed on the spirit of selfless service which is an enduring and veritable possession'.

Miss Finlay, herself, speaking of her recollections of the school in 1971 emphasised the family atmosphere which she found when she became Headmistress in 1916, and Miss Mowbray's keen participation in all aspects of school life. Miss Mowbray was an enthusiastic botanist and used to take the children for 'botanical walks' in the water meadows; she was full of encouragement for games and used to watch matches with extreme interest; music was a particular pleasure to her, but central to her whole work in the school was her profound regard for 'sound learning and service to God', and it is singularly appropriate that the school's most distinguished academic to date, Dr. Jocelyn Toynbee, should have started on her career as a classical scholar in that year by winning Classical Scholarships to both Girton and to Newnham, her mother's old college, where she chose to go.

III

Miss Finlay 1916-1940

1916-1929

Miss Finlay came to Winchester from Cheltenham Ladies College where she had been teaching for the last four years, and where she had also been educated before going to St Hilda's, Oxford, to read Modern History. She was 34 years old and was chosen from 54 applicants. The war was well into its second year and food shortages and rising prices added to the anxieties of a new Headmistress: the Housemistresses were asking whether they could charge extra fees, as food prices were rising all the time, and later in 1916 Miss Finlay herself asked the Council to consider paying a war bonus to the staff as was being done in other schools, because of the increased cost of living and travelling.

Both these increases were agreed, but food shortages remained. Ethel Rosser wrote 'Sugar and jam were scarce and we had a curious substitute called Honey Sugar. I think we could only manage to get meat twice a week and we consumed quantities of lentils. Cakes of any kind were a rare treat, and few in quality and variety'. She also described an experience which must have been only too common. 'During the Easter holidays of 1916 Arthur [her brother] came home on leave from France and there was great rejoicing in the family. He had ten days leave from the trenches and we had a gay time together. I had to return to school before it was over but my Parents and Hester went to London for the last few days with him. The leave trains always left to go back to France at night from Victoria or Charing Cross Station. His was Victoria Station and when my Parents sadly waved the train out they were convinced that they would never see him again. I imagine everybody who saw off a leave train in those days had a similar feeling. It couldn't be otherwise for the slaughter was ghastly. Nothing like it happened in the Second World War.

'They were right. On July the First the Battle of the Somme started and on the tenth the 38th Division, the Welsh Regiment, went into action at Mametz Wood. The survivors were few. A few days afterwards came the dreaded telegram "missing believed killed". My mother had gone out but something told her to go back home at once and she arrived at the front door at the same moment as the telegraph boy. My father came to Winchester to tell me and take me home. It was the day before the School Certificate examination was to have started; for that reason I never took it. For some months there was always the hope in my Parents' minds that Arthur, aged 19, would eventually turn up, perhaps even as a prisoner of war. Enquiries were made through the Red Cross but there was no trace of him, and no body or remains of a body were ever found. He must have been blown to bits. My Parents never fully got over their misery. My Father wore a black tie to the end of his life. Arthur had given my Mother a gold regimental brooch, the three feathers of the Welsh Regiment. It was the fashion in those days, and the brooches were bought at Packers in Regent Street. She wore that brooch as her only piece of jewellery until the outbreak of the Second World War'.

25

The war affected the life of the school in lesser ways as well. The playing fields were used by troops for sports, and while there were Canadians stationed in Winchester the school played an occasional game of lacrosse with them. Miss Bramston and Miss LeRoy were much involved in work for the many Belgian refugees in and near Winchester (for which they were decorated at the end of the war) and the school helped to entertain them, notably at Christmas, and raised money for their needs. A recurring note in the Headmistress's Reports for 1917 and 1918 is the amount of illness and infection in the town, and anxiety about the desirability of restricting the girls' contacts. Of 'war work' as known to girls who were at school during the Second World War there is little mention, although in 1917 the possibility of some of the older girls taking part in light agricultural work was explored, and in 1918 the senior girls and staff found themselves involved in the issue of ration books for the whole population of Winchester.

One of the most profound effects of the war on this generation of schoolgirls arose from the sheer need of the country for more labour, which could only be supplied by women when all able-bodied men were recruited into the armed forces. This, though it was probably not recognised at the time, was a far more powerful influence on the 'liberation' of women than all the efforts of the educationalists and suffragettes had been. Hints of the changes to come began to appear in the school by the middle of the war. In 1916 the government circularised schools, asking them to provide some systematic secretarial training for girls, to offset the severe shortage of male clerical officers. This was easily organised as the school secretary had for some years been giving some instruction, but progress for larger numbers was rather hampered by there being only one typewriter available.

In her first Headmistress's Report Miss Finlay wrote of an increasing interest in careers attributable to the conditions of war, and at the Old Girls' Meeting in 1917 she included the following passage in her speech:

> Just from the pleasure of earning, and the excitement of doing something for the country at once, girls are running into 'blind alley employments', which must from their very nature be temporary, and by breaking into serious training are depriving the country of the trained, well-educated women who will be required more than ever in the future. I am glad to say that two of our present girls are intending to go to Oxford to study Economics, and I hope there will be more. There is little room for amateurs in these days, and since women will be called upon to play a bigger part in days to come, we must see that they are fit to do it.

Because of an agreeable custom established by Miss Mowbray, girls in the school during the war years got to know the kind of work women were undertaking through letters to the *Chronicle* from Old Girls, and this may well have been partly responsible for stimulating the interest in careers of which Miss Finlay wrote. One example was the letter written in 1916 by Enid Whitmore-Smith:

> For the first year of the War I remained at home, but later I went down to Vickers' at Erith, and started munition work. The people who originally started the scheme, did so with the idea of providing weekend relief work for the ordinary factory girls, and for some time I did that—just at the weekend. Later, Vickers' started a plan by which two people were allowed to share a lathe, each doing alternate weeks. I did that for a while, and then took another course of training, and am now certificated to be able to do 'accurate plain turning', i.e., work to 1000th of an inch, if need be. I was always one of the most inaccurate of mortals, so it was very good for my character! I left Vickers' in April, as they started the twelve-hour shift instead of eight, and it was rather much. Also, there was nowhere down there to live, and with that kind of work one must be able to come

back to a certain amount of luxury. They sent six of us up to Glasgow in April to help teach the girls in a new factory for 6in. shells. It was frightfully interesting, and we had the time of our lives. It was quite an experience.

I came to my present job in May, and hope to stick to it as long as it sticks to me. I now work at a garage in Buckingham Gate, which is making munitions—quite a small place, only twelve lathes, but we turn out 1500 nose-pieces for the high explosive 4.5 shells per week. We work from 8 a.m. to 6.30 p.m., with an hour off for lunch, and the night shift the same. There are only three women, and the rest are men. We have from 1 o'clock Saturday and all Sunday off, so it really is an ideal job of its kind. So many of these places are in such terrible surroundings; also being partly a garage we get a lot more fresh air than usual. I am very happy at it. The only thing is that it will not lead to any permanent work after the War.

Lieba Buckley, who had embarked on an academic career as a junior don at Girton just before the War, wrote of her experiences as a radiographer at Royaumont in France, in one of the first hospitals sent out by the Scottish Women's Hospitals for Foreign Service. 'They were staffed entirely by women, and were in the first instance offered to the British Red Cross, but were refused because in the early days the War Office had not felt the need of women doctors. Thus it was that they worked for the French, Serbs, Russians and Roumanians from their several inceptions throughout the war. Royaumont was started in November 1914, in the ancient Abbaye of that name, founded in 1120 by St Louis...right in the depths of the country. The nearest town of any size was Chantilly, six miles away, where the French Headquarters were for so many months. Our wounded—French, Arab, and Senegalese N.C.O.s and men—came by train to Creil, a large station on the Paris-Boulogne line, twelve miles away from us, whence they were conveyed in ambulances by our chauffeurs, office staff, and oddments, such as myself...'

'During the winter of 1915-6 the trains of the wounded came in more or less regularly, twice a week, at nights. A telephone message used to come through to send so many cars—"quinze blesses, neuf assis, six couches". As they arrived at the hall doors a whistle was blown; all the surgeons came down, also the orderlies on duty. The orderlies helped the chauffeurs to lift the stretchers out and put them in rows in the hall, the walkers being assisted to seats. The head surgeon apportioned them to the various wards, and then the orderlies carried them off to their respective receiving rooms. We had up to nine or ten wards in use at times, especially after we were increased to 400 beds, an event which happened, I believe, somewhere in 1916. They were mainly named after famous women, from Blanche de Castille to Millicent Fawcett. These ladies were always known familiarly by their Christian names.

'The Abbaye was built round a square cloister; we had anything up to 100 beds out there in the summer of 1916. The men loved it and many of their own choice stayed out there into the beginning of winter. In times of great pressure the beautiful old refectory was also made into a ward of 80 beds, and we fed in the cloisters. One year we went on with this plan until the beginning of December; it was then so cold that everyone put her hands into her pockets between each mouthful, and "dressing for dinner" meant turning up to supper in every conceivable garment one could lay hands on. After that an old Cinema Palace was requisitioned and dumped outside the kitchen door as a dining room for the sisters and orderlies, while the rest of us had the linen room. Those of us who were doctors, or classed for convenience as such, had a sitting-room on the first floor, where we had breakfast and tea. The sisters had a room next door, and the orderlies had first one and then two sitting-rooms as their numbers increased.

'The sleeping accommodation was at times pretty crowded. The doctors had a cell each. Some of the more senior sisters and orderlies shared a cell between two. The remainder slept in "barns" or cubicles, which were very noisy. All the bedroom furniture was made by us out of packing cases. There were singularly few arrangements for heating in any part of the hospital, except the stoves we had placed in the wards. The underground system of drainage was, we were creditably informed, the same as that originally laid down by St. Louis' workmen, but it served its purpose very well. Several times a year it had to be cleaned out. On these occasions one had, if possible, an important commission in Paris, or failing that, an afternoon off'.

The war years saw many changes in the structure of the school. The resignation of Mrs. Wood from Earlsdown led to the appointment of Miss Weston as the first salaried housemistress, relieved of any financial responsibility for her house, and her appointment was quickly followed by that of Miss Gregory in Hyde Abbey. Mrs. Carbery moved Hillcroft up on to St Giles Hill at the beginning of 1918, which enabled her to take in some extra girls, an urgent necessity as numbers had grown from 146 to over 200 in the first two years of Miss Finlay's headship. For the first time, potential boarders had to be refused (in the autumn term of 1918) and thereafter hardly a term passed until the school moved to its present site without some problem relating to the pressure of numbers being discussed in Council Meetings. As a first step to try to relieve the problem, a fifth boarding house, North Hill House in the Andover Road, was opened in 1919 and shortly turned into a Junior boarding house, the forerunner of LeRoy.

A more radical change, however, took place in 1919. Since its inception the school had been in receipt of a grant from the Board of Education, and now, owing to a change in regulations, it was faced with two alternatives. Either it could guarantee a number of 'free places', give no denominational religious teaching except on request, and impose no denominational requirements on either the Headmistress or the Members of the Council (a third of whom would be nominated by the Local Education Authority), in which case it would be entitled to receive an increased grant from the Board; or it could forego all grants and retain its present character and future independence. It was unanimously agreed that the second of these alternatives was preferable, and thereafter the school has received no grant, though protracted negotiations with the Board allowed it to be included in the government's superannuation scheme.

During the war the Old Girls' meetings were severely curtailed, and it was not until 1918 that the question of a memorial to Miss Mowbray's period as Headmistress was discussed. It was suggested (as it turned out, rather optimistically) that it might take the form of contributions towards a new hall, to be called the Mowbray Hall, or else towards the establishment of a Mowbray Scholarship. After various abortive proposals had been put forward, and there had been a certain amount of disagreement, a prayer desk was the final choice, together with the establishment of a loan bursary to be drawn upon either by girls going to college, or to enable girls to spend an extra year at school which financial considerations would otherwise have denied them.

By 1921 the school had more or less recovered from the effects of the war. It had acquired a telephone, although this was at a time when the relative merits of a brougham or a landau as a conveyance for sick children to the Sanatorium could still be a matter for discussion, and in 1920 the whole school seems to have been thrown into a turmoil of excitement by two days of lectures on wireless telegraphy. During the course of practical demonstrations, the lecturer, Major Lefroy, made contact with Berlin, America and the Eiffel Tower. Lectures and musical events had been restored to the school's calendar during the course of 1919. In 1922 both W.B. Yeats and Alfred Noyes gave talks at the school.

Of the school's various societies, the Science Society was particularly active under the guidance of Miss Verinder: in 1921 girls read papers on 'Science and the War', 'Waves', and 'The Life and Work of John Dalton'. In the holidays six girls spent a fortnight at Studley Agricultural College.

More relaxing leisure activities were not forgotten either. A request made by Miss Finlay to the Council in 1922 reminds us that staff as well as girls were probably largely dependent on what the school could provide for entertainment, and were certainly subject to considerable control over their activities in term-time. In her Report to the Council of 9 February 1922 Miss Finlay wrote 'The last point to be mentioned may seem frivolous, but I believe it is an important matter concerning the welfare of the Staff. The mistresses have formed a dancing class with my full approval. Would the Council sanction outsiders coming to this?'. They did!

Although by this time the school did possess a member of staff specially appointed to oversee games, the staff as a whole still took a considerable part in coaching, and during the early 1920s their efforts must have borne some fruit, for in 1924 a girl was sent to take part in the Southern Counties lacrosse trials for the first time, and won a place in the team.

On the academic side there is plenty of information, as the school had another general inspection in 1921 from which it emerged with much credit. The main teaching was still confined to the morning between 9.00 and 12.50 though there were some special classes during the afternoon. Standards were still high; the inspectors remarked that soft options were discouraged, indeed were not allowed, and if a faint note of criticism creeps in when it is observed that so many exacting subjects are taught that the time allowed for any one subject seems rather inadequate, nevertheless they are able to note that 'it is not usual to find Mathematics so seriously treated in a girl's school' and to praise the staff—'there are few schools which can claim to have a more highly qualified or a more competent body of mistresses'. They concluded that the school was undoubtedly one where the intellectual girl had her opportunity, yet the girl of no great intellectual parts was also amply provided for. On all sides there seemed to be genuine work, conscientiously done. 'There is a very pleasant atmosphere about the school—a happy combination of simplicity, seriousness and refinement'.

The academic world was also beginning to recognise the calibre of the Staff. In 1921 Miss Finlay was appointed to the Executive of the Headmistresses' Association, and later became President of the Six Counties Branch. She and Miss Clark represented Hampshire on the Joint Four Committee, and Miss Clark and Miss Verinder were respectively President and Secretary of the Hampshire Branch of the Assistant Mistresses Association. Miss Clark gained a further recognition as a result of the general inspection; she was invited to lecture at a course in Eastbourne, supported by the Board of Education, in mathematics.

The inspectors remarked that the school accommodation, though excellent, seemed to have reached its limit, and in particular that additional laboratory space was needed as there was only one small one for the whole school. It may well have been these observations which caused the Council to begin negotiations in the following year for the purchase of Northgate House, next door to the existing school buildings. The sale was not finally agreed until the end of 1923, when it was bought for £3,600. The house was quickly transformed into four new classrooms, three music rooms and living accommodation for Miss Finlay, and it was found possible to make two new tennis courts out of the garden. Thus for a little while the worst pressures on the school were removed, but one part of the newly acquired property was to give rise to a controversy which troubled the school for many years—should the school have its own chapel or not?

Miss Finlay was clearly very keen that it should, and within six months of the acquisition of Northgate House, she raised the matter with the Council, suggesting that it might be possible to convert the garage into a chapel, and asking that she might mention the matter on Parents Day with a view to opening a fund. This was going a little too fast for some of the Council, who felt that the matter needed much thought and that it bristled with difficulties, financial, structural and ecclesiastical. Neverthe-less, it was agreed that the Council would view any reasonable scheme with sympathy, and Miss Finlay was given discretion as to whether to mention it on Parents Day. She evidently did, and again also at the Old Girls' Annual Meeting, when it was enthusiastically welcomed and a Chapel Fund set up.

At the beginning of 1925 Miss Finlay again brought the matter to the Council's notice by producing two architects' schemes and tentative estimates; once again members of the Council seem to have felt that their hand was being slightly forced by an over-eager Headmistress. However, they continued to discuss the possibilities for the next year and a half, during which time it became clear that there were a substantial number of the Council who did not really see the need for a school chapel, and indeed thought that they might be exceeding their powers in sanctioning the building of one. Even amongst those who were not wholly opposed to a chapel, there was a division between those who thought that only a really beautiful building should be allowed, and those who felt the matter to be so urgent that a less fine, or even a temporary building would be sufficient, if this would ease the financial problem.

In the end, after an exhaustive and somewhat heated discussion by the Council in June 1926, it was clear that the members were almost equally divided for and against the building, and a large majority voted for a resolution that 'the Council finds it impossible to proceed with any scheme for the purpose for at least the next two years'. In the event the matter was not raised again immediately at the end of the two year period, and then the Council's energies were shortly directed to much more ambitious and far-reaching building schemes. In the meantime Miss Finlay was left to make what arrangements seemed best to her for the money so far collected towards the chapel; contributions towards the Fund were suspended for two years and began again in 1928, when it stood at about £500.

In 1927 the school's name was finally changed to St Swithun's after discussions lasting on and off for eight years and its present motto was chosen. The statue of St Swithun which now stands on the main staircase was commissioned from Captain Basil Gotto in memory of Anne Hagedon, a boarder who died in 1929. In 1936 a Grant of Arms was made, and the school acquired its own Coat of Arms.

Time was running out for the old school building in North Walls. A combination of circumstances in 1929 led to the Council's decision to move from the site. There was much illness in the Spring Term; Miss Finlay in her Report to the Council said 'this has been a sick term', and asked that it might end early to give staff as well as girls a chance to recover from the debilitating effects of illness; but the Summer Term too had its share of sickness. Then, after Parents' Day, Miss Finlay had a letter from a parent:

> We walked round the playing field afterwards and seeing land for sale, longed for the School Council to see a vision, and build up there really adequate school buildings. Three really desirable families have been recommended by us to send their girls to Winchester, and they have all turned it down because of the position of the school buildings; it is such a waste of time going backwards and forwards.

Miss Finlay quoted this letter in her Report to the Council in July, and added that the school was still having problems in accommodating all the girls who wanted to come, particularly boarders. When the Council came to discuss the matter, the Headmistress told them that the traffic down North Walls and the consequent noise was becoming almost unbearable, and on that account she had the greatest difficulty persuading parents to send their children to her. While no immediate decision was taken, several members of the Council agreed to make a tour of some girls' public schools to look at their buildings. When Council met again in October, having heard Miss Finlay's considered view that the move was desirable, and that the Treasurer thought it financially possible, the decision in favour of the move was unanimous.

1929-1940

As yet, of course, there was no certainty that a site was available. Some 20 acres of land adjacent to the existing playing field and Sanatorium were for sale by the Ecclesiastical Commissioners. The Treasurer—Mr. Madams—was empowered to negotiate for the purchase of the land. There was a degree of urgency, since the by-pass was already scheduled, and it was thought that the land might become more sought-after and valuable because of this. Nevertheless a good deal of hard bargaining went on as the school was obviously reluctant to raise a larger sum than was absolutely necessary. In the course of this Miss Finlay was asked to produce a memorandum for the Church Commissioners pointing out that St Swithun's was a church school without any endowments, and giving some account of the contribution made to national and church life by the Old Girls of the school.

In the spring of 1930 a price of £110 an acre was finally agreed upon, making the total cost of the land £3,300. The first tentative estimate of the cost of the whole operation had been £40,000, but it quickly became clear that £50,000 was a more realistic figure, and this amount was accepted shortly afterwards. The Annual Report of the School Association of 27 November 1929 contained the first public announcement of the school's intention. As soon as the news was out the sale of the old school premises could be undertaken, and by May 1930 it was agreed that an offer of £15,000 could be accepted. At the same time the Council decided to buy the Old Golf House for £975 as a house for the Headmistress.

The next step was to find an architect and builders. The architects chosen were a young firm, Messrs. Mitchell and Bridgewater of Hanover Square, London, who had already had some experience in designing school buildings. Drawings of their whole scheme show the central teaching block flanked by two double boarding houses with two more facing them across the playing fields, the whole linked together by a covered way which was broken on the short east side by a chapel. Provision was also made for a Headmistress's house.

The first formal ceremony connected with the new buildings was the laying of the foundation stone on 31 October 1930 by the then Bishop of Winchester, Bishop

Theodore Woods. During a short service the stone was lowered into place, and in a cavity behind it was placed a bottle containing a copy of the Articles of Association of the school, the front page of the current issue of *The Times*, and some coins. This was the last public occasion on which Miss Bramston was to be present—she had helped to cut the first turf in a private ceremony a few weeks earlier—as very sadly she died on 23 January 1931, aged 83, having devoted the whole of her life from the age of 36 to the school of which she was the foundress.

Dr. Davies, the Chairman of the Council, wrote of her in the *Chronicle*:

If living in its best and truest sense is the successful development of some good and noble plan, Miss Bramston, on the Eve of All Saint's Day 1930, when she was present at the laying of the Foundation Stone of our new school, could have asserted with deep satisfaction, 'I have lived'.

This was only one of many tributes paid to her by local people and organisations, all of whom spoke of her selflessness. In a sermon preached in the city two days after her death, the Rev. J.H.R. Mace said 'It would be impossible to say all she has been to those engaged in the work of the School and what they owe to her wise and understanding mind or how she treated them all as personal friends, making them feel she cared for them. I have seldom met so broadminded a soul, for she was always ready and anxious to learn new things right up to the end, even when those new things upset what she held'. Miss Finlay, who must have known her as intimately as anyone, spoke about her at some length when she came to record her memories of the school in her own old age, saying that she believed Miss Bramston's life had been given to God and her fellow beings.

She was the daughter of Dean Bramston and, from the beginning of her wishes about the school, he gave her his support in every way he could; and her great friend [Miss LeRoy] who is sometimes considered a co-founder—but I think she was hardly that—was a lifelong companion. She [Miss LeRoy] had come to England, having French parents, at the age of five, and at some time in the early period of her life she and Miss Bramston met and made a life-long friendship, and they made their home Witham Close the resting place—one might say the healing place—for a great many in Winchester. Their life was one of service to their fellows and I should think they very rarely had a meal alone. I have never forgotten their welcome to me on the day I was appointed and I spent my first night in Winchester at Witham Close, and from that moment they were my most steadfast friends and critics, which was really very helpful. They quite openly criticised changes that had to be made in the school, but they never interfered. Miss Bramston was Honorary Secretary almost up to the day of her death, and she paid frequent—daily—visits to the school, and curiously enough, it was the Honorary Secretary who, in those days, gave a report on the school to the Council, not the Headmistress, and she was in with every single move in the school.

She knew the Staff intimately. They entertained the girls; they had a Sunday lunch to which the seniors were invited in turn at Witham Close. It was, indeed, a social centre for the school, and for a great many others, because Miss Bramston was not only interested in the school but she was intensely interested in the city, and she was President of the Women's Citizens Association in Winchester, and she was also President of the local branch of the National Council of Women and—I wish I could remember the occasion—I remember the sight in the Town Hall when they were celebrating some particular thing in the City, when Miss Bramston made a walk round the Hall and she was greeted with cheers. It was not very long before her death, but I can still see that little upright figure, rather stern-faced, clad in black silk brocade, beautiful little lace cap on her head, and carrying a long black stick with a silver top, and as she walked round the room they cheered and cheered...She really stole the evening.

Her activities extended not only to places in the school or in the city arrangements, it was nothing uncommon in winter months to meet her coming along Kingsgate Street carrying a basket or small crate of coal to some person who had no firing, as she was completely selfless as far as onlookers could tell.

I know some people found her criticism hard to bear as she was very downright in her remarks. You can't possibly think of Miss Bramston without Miss LeRoy because they were so much at one, and it was interesting to see how the rather severe outlook on life of one was lightened by the other with a Gallic temperament. Witham Close was the place where people of all ages—all types—could expect a welcome and understanding.

Old Girls and members of the Staff who remember Miss Bramston mainly came into contact with her through her custom of inviting them to lunch on Sunday, and they mostly remember it as an awe-inspiring and formal occasion, the two elderly ladies rather stern and critical in black, the maids in long black dresses and white caps with long white 'streamers', the anxieties about table manners lightened in one case by the remembrance of the custom of placing a little nosegay by each place at the table which could be taken away at the end of the meal.

Although the Council had so far only undertaken to build a new teaching block for the school, it was realised that removal up the hill would pose problems for the boarders living in the houses in the town, Hyde Abbey and North Hill House, such as had previously been faced by those on Morn Hill. Both of these houses were in need of modernisation and were leasehold property (Earlsdown and High House had been bought outright by the school in 1929). Parents did not like the long treks girls had to make to and from lessons and games, and there was in any case an urgent need for more boarding space. Thus it came about that the full boarding operations envisaged by Messrs. Mitchell and Butler included new boarding houses, and early in 1931 the Council was being pressed by Miss Finlay to embark on the building of some boarding accommodation as soon as possible. As a result a special sub-committee was set up in April 1931 to consider the proposal, and at the same time a decision was taken about the appointment of housemistresses which was to bring the school more in line with current practice in other girls' public schools. Hitherto their role had been purely pastoral; now when vacancies occurred the new appointments were to be of women who would also teach part-time. (Some seven years earlier the school had taken another step which emphasised its public school character by appointing its first prefects to take on duties previously shared amongst all members of the Upper VI.)

At the end of the summer term of 1931 the school said goodbye to its old buildings on North Walls. The move itself took place in the summer holidays with many members of the staff giving up part of their own holiday to help. Miss Finlay wrote in the 1934 *History*:

That work began punctually in the new buildings on September 24th, 1931, was due to our architects and our contractors, Messrs. Chapman, Lowry, and Puttick. The equanimity and good humour of all those concerned in those first few weeks, when doors were still lacking and stairs impassable, and laboratories were incomplete owing to a sectional strike, was beyond all praise. In addition to those difficulties, the building was almost besieged by the interested and the curious, many having seen Mr. Bridgwater's drawing of the School in the Royal Academy, and these expected admission at all hours and on every day of the week.

On 2 October the Bishop of Winchester informally opened the school, processing through it and dedicating it 'To the glory of God and the education of His children'. The Quiet Room was specially dedicated; its furnishings and plate were in part given in memory of Mary Irving, a former head girl, who had been killed climbing with her fiancé in the Alps during the summer of 1930, immediately after she had left school. The flèche and the clock it contains were the gift of the Old Girls and Staff in memory of Miss Bramston. The new Hall was also named after her, and a bust of her, given by Miss LeRoy (who survived her by only a year) was placed in the Library.

The formal opening did not take place until the following spring when on 10 Mary 1932 the Princess Royal visited the school. As with all royal visits the amount of preparation involved was considerable: movements round the school, presentations, timing, photographs, all had to be precisely organised as well as the wellbeing of all the guests. Miss Finlay's file of all the details is a large one, and includes her correspondence with the then Headmistress of Headington School, who had recently had such a visit and who could give her many useful pieces of advice such as where to walk in relation to the royal visitor. As she quite rightly said in one letter to Miss Finlay 'I think these little things make all the difference to one's sense of security'.

When the day finally arrived, it was tinged with sadness, as the Bishop of Winchester (Bishop Woods) who had been such a friend to the school, had died only the previous week; but apart from this all seems to have gone well. The Princess duly opened the front door with a gilt key contained in a silver casket, which was presented to her by the architect, Mr. Mitchell. A short service took place in the Hall at which the Choir sang an anthem which had been specially composed for the opening of the new Hall at Queen Anne's, Caversham, three years earlier. Speeches followed: the Princess did not make one as she was very shy in public, but she did declare the school open, and added that she had asked the Headmistress for an extra four days holiday for the school which caused much applause.

The distinguished visitors were served tea in the Library by senior girls, and all the Staff were presented. After touring a good part of the new building the Princess left, watched and cheered by the whole school. It was generally agreed that although she appeared rather formal in public the Princess had been more relaxed and keenly interested as she toured the school. Miss Finlay wrote:

> Space does not permit a full account of the visit of the Princess Royal; mention can only be made of her graciousness and keen interest in everything noticeable from the moment of her arrival: her real pleasure in the gift of the architects, a finely carved silver box holding the gold key for the door, the massed flowers in the Entrance Hall, the working of the thermostats, the modelling of the Juniors, her joy in the views—nothing escaped her notice, and her last words asked for an assurance that the holiday she had requested would be granted. The Downs were a wonderful sight, packed with cars and loyal onlookers, and the weather being kind the whole School was able to turn out and give the Princess a great send-off. A great day in the annals of the School, and following this gracious visit came at Christmas time a kind message of remembrance and a portrait of the Princess Royal which now hangs in the entrance hall.

In her first Report to the Council after the move, Miss Finlay observed 'It only needed the new traffic regulations in last week's local paper ordaining that the main stream should pass down North Walls to emphasise the need of this move. All are benefiting already from the good air, the quiet, proper heating and space'. She went on, however 'While observing enthusiastically on the new building and site, parents are asking about the first new Boarding House' and indeed it soon became clear that parents were increasingly reluctant to enter their daughters for the two houses down in the town.

The effects of the Wall Street Crash of 1929 were by this time being strongly felt in Britain, and this inevitably added to the school's problems. It was operating in an increasingly competitive market where parents wanted real value for money: this it felt it could give academically, but materially there could be no such certainty. Nevertheless, it had already borrowed heavily to build the teaching block: the total cost of the new building had been £48,352, and of that total £40,000 had been borrowed incurring an annual liability of just over £3,000. It was hoped to fund this out of the school's annual surplus, and here the problem came full circle, for in order to achieve a sufficient surplus the school had to be full, and in order to be full it had to attract parents...

In 1933, therefore, the Council began to explore the possible cost of building a double boarding house and possible means of financing the project. They were experiencing difficulty in obtaining the full amount of the sale of the old school building, as the purchaser himself had been affected by the economic situation, and indeed the school did not receive the full price until the end of the 1930s. State controlled schools imposed a 10% salary cut on all their staff at this time, and the staff at St Swithun's voluntarily accepted a like cut to try to ease the school's position. Taking all these factors into account it was decided that the Council should go ahead with the building of a double boarding house at an estimated total cost of £24,000, funding it with a £16,000 loan and an £8,000 bank overdraft, the building to be complete by the beginning of 1934.

Nor was this the end of the building programme. The school had had to use the public swimming baths for many years after a kind but temporary loan of the College's facilities for a few years after the First World War. Pressure from parents for the school to have its own pool had been increasing. With the school now up the hill, the inconvenience of using the public pool was increased, and with the help of two endowment policies which were about to fall due, the decision was taken in February 1935 to install a swimming bath.

Decision on the matter was probably somewhat delayed as in 1934 the school was giving most of its attention to another matter—its 50th Anniversary celebrations. The boarding houses were finished (slightly late) in January 1934, and after some thought and consultation with the Old Girls it was decided to keep the old house names (High House and Hyde Abbey). The old North Hill house which was moving into the old High House, and becoming a junior house was, however, renamed 'LeRoy' 'in memory of the great work Miss LeRoy had done for the school, in conjunction with Miss Bramston'. Happily, Miss LeRoy lived to know of this, though she died shortly after the opening of the new boarding houses on 12 March 1934. Although her service to the school was not as immediately obvious as that of Miss Bramston, yet much of the thought and planning that went into the first 50 years of St Swithun's was their joint product. They were joint hostesses at Witham Close, and, as someone wrote, Miss LeRoy, although she had left France at the age of five, always retained a faint accent, a French elegance and a Gallic wit to lighten the rather more severe outlook of her companion.

The Jubilee Celebrations were contained within the weekend of 14-18 June, during the whole of which time, according to the *Hampshire Chronicle*, the weather was lovely. The first major event of the weekend was a service in the Cathedral on the Friday evening, at which the Bishop of Winchester was the preacher, on the text 'Praise ye the Lord: Praise God in His Sanctuary. Praise Him in the firmament of His power. Praise Him in His mighty acts'. He reminded the congregation that they had come together to praise God for their school. When reading its history, he felt that two words stood out, 'Vision' and 'Courage', and that three women in particular had possessed these qualities, Anna Bramston, Aimée LeRoy and Margaret Mowbray. On

Saturday morning there was a special Eucharist for the school, the Old Girls, parents and friends, at which they could offer their thanks for the first 50 years of the school.

A strong element in all such celebrations is the opportunity to reminisce, and there was certainly plenty of time at the Old Girls' dinner on Friday evening, when nearly 300 people, including representatives of the Council, past members of staff, and the Head Girl and her six prefects sat down to dinner in the Bramston Hall. There was public reminiscing in the speeches, notably that of Sir Edward Altham—the father of a present member of Council—who proposed the toast to the Council, appropriately since he had known six of its original 12 members personally; in his speech he made plain how close the school's connection with the College had been from the very beginning. (This seems a suitable place to record a charming story told about Sir Edward by his daughter. He was a great cricketer, and for some years helped to coach the St Swithun's girls. At the end of one session, indicating one young woman, he remarked that she was coming along quite nicely and should be worth a place in the team in a year or two—only to discover that she was the Junior Games Mistress.)

A former member of staff, in proposing the health of the Staff, had some good stories about Miss Mowbray; as did an Old Girl proposing the health of her fellows—Miss Mowbray characteristically terse in a Scripture lesson 'We shall have to alter that because a new King of Assyria was discovered during the vacation' and giving advice to a member of staff going to an interview 'Remember, when you are interviewed, to see that your braid is well stitched on to your skirt, and that you have no holes in your gloves' and prophetically in 1915 when delivering a new girl to High House 'We simply must move up here to this hill some day'.

Saturday was given over primarily to the present members of school, their parents and guests, who numbered nearly a thousand persons, and in the afternoon there was another round of speeches. Sir Charles Grant Robertson, substituting at short notice for the Warden of New College, Oxford, H.A.L. Fisher, who had forgotten to write the date down in his diary, spoke most compellingly on the revolution contained in the changed conception of the status and part which women played and could play between 1884 and 1934, which was perhaps summed up by the remark of a boy who was beaten by a girl in an examination. When his father said 'Fancy being beaten by a mere girl' the boy replied 'Father, girls aren't so mere as they were in your day'.

On Saturday evening the school gave a performance of J.M. Barrie's *Quality Street*: as one critic observed, an appropriate choice for an occasion which must hold many memories. Many of the Old Girls stayed on through Sunday, which was a day for more relaxed enjoyment and celebration.

One topic which emerged again during the preparations for the Jubilee, and the discussions of the possible objects for an appeal, was the idea of a school chapel, which had been in abeyance since a difficult Council meeting in June 1926. The Old Girls Association continued to ask for it to be built, and still contributed to the fund. During 1936 and 1937 the Council gave a good deal of thought to the matter, and in March 1937 a special sub-committee recommended the building of a chapel, which should cost not more than £3,000 in the first instance. It was to consist of a permanent east end with a temporary body which would be capable of being extended when money became available. It was not until the summer of 1938, however, that a sufficient measure of agreement amongst Council members was reached, to allow two sketches of the first, and of the final, stages of the building to be exhibited on Parents' Day, and to be published in the 1937-8 issue of the *Chronicle*. An appeal was sent out to all parents to try and raise the £800 needed to reach the sum of £8,000, but by Parents' Day 1939 this sum had still not been achieved—and by that time parents and school alike had other preoccupations.

Through the memories of present members of the Old Girls Association, it is possible to build up quite a detailed picture of what it was like to be a pupil at St Swithun's during the 1930s. For the junior and middle schools, the majority of lessons were still contained in the morning with 'extra' subjects only spilling over into the afternoon, but by 1936 the senior forms were being taught on a regular basis on some afternoons in the week. Staff were teaching on two afternoons a week and many of the younger ones were also helping with games on other days.

The boarders walked to school from their various houses in crocodile with the juniors on the outside of the pavement. If adults were met or overtaken, the rule was that ladies were allowed the inside of the pavement, men had to get past on the outside, but if a lady with a pram was encountered, the whole crocodile stepped into the road. The girls walked two and two, but if there was an uneven number in the crocodile the unfortunate one who was left without a partner had to ask another pair if she could 'tag' with them. One new girl remembers committing the unwitting sin of asking a senior if she could 'tag'. While the school was still down in the town, a 'satchel-cart' used to go down from St Giles Hill taking all the satchels, and occasionally giving a lift to those who needed it. Day girls got to school by a variety of means; a special school bus, bicycles, and one Old Girl remembers some of her contemporaries being brought by nannies.

Academic work was clearly well and vigorously taught, but one gets the impression that it was not regarded as overwhelmingly important as it was in the school's earlier years. Several Old Girls of that period felt that for the majority of girls neither the necessity nor the desirability of having a career and earning their own living was strongly felt, though the appreciation of good teaching was clearly there. A number of staff stood out for their ability and personality: Miss Debes, later Mrs. Claye, universally popular and inspiring as a history teacher; Miss Verinder, a marvellous if demanding teacher of science, who left to become headmistress of St Cyprian's School, Cape Town; Miss Clark, herself an Old Girl, who could teach almost anyone mathematics—described by one of her ex-pupils as 'a flash of teeth and spectacles'—and Miss Pym, also an Old Girl, whose lessons on Shakespeare are often remembered. Miss Armit who taught Classics was a figure who inspired general awe, but to one girl, taught by her at Lower VI level, she 'unbent a little, showing the great charm that to those lower in the School was always disguised under the role of arch-martinet'. At this time the Staff gave up a good deal of their free time to the school, and were expected to do so; one member remembers Miss Finlay being very unwilling for her to run an outside Guide company. One of the ways in which they contributed to school life during the 1930s was by a series of plays they put on, which were clearly much appreciated by the school at the time.

Games played a considerable part in school life, and were played by many every afternoon. The Senior Games Staff throughout this period was Miss Snowball, who was Vice-Captain of the English Women's Cricket Team which toured Australia in 1934. One of her deputies was Miss Ashdown, who created something of a sensation by coming to work on a motor-cycle complete with leather coat and crash helmet: she was inevitably nicknamed 'Crashdown'. The chief games played were lacrosse in the winter and cricket in the summer, together with some tennis. While they gave great pleasure to those who were good at them, they naturally also bulk large in the memories of those who did not enjoy them. One Old Girl writes:

> No doubt for those really good at games it was enjoyable (I did, eventually, rise to the dizzy heights of the second lacrosse team and it was much more fun then). But for the ungifted, who were put down on the remote and less good pitches, where there was rarely any coaching and the ball, owing to our ineptitude, usually on the ground, it was a cold and dreary ordeal. Cricket games were less traumatic, and at least it was usually warm; but being stuck sometimes at the far end of a practice net, with ferocious women launching fast balls at one could be an alarming experience. We did play tennis sometimes.

Another Old Girl remembers deliberately arranging as many piano practices as possible during the afternoon and as she later became a music teacher remarks 'You could say that I took up Music to avoid playing Cricket'.

During the 1930s the school uniform was changed in colour from navy to its present brown, and those who experienced this change seem to regard it generally with disfavour. The reason for it was apparently pressure by a number of parents for clothes, and particularly for coats, which the girls could wear in the holidays, thus obviating the necessity for two expensive outfits at a time when money was universally short. One can only suppose that they were remarkably optimistic and naive if they supposed that any schoolgirl would wear school uniform out of term time. However, Miss Finlay acceded to these requests, and of the navy blue only the gym tunics remained. Previously hats had had interchangeable bands, with house and school colours, which seem to have been a matter of some pride, and there were also house and school ties and—evidently objects of some envy and admiration—gold ties for members of first school teams.

For boarders life in their Houses was at least as important as the school day, and they tended to be very closeknit communities, provoking one Old Girl to write 'Day girls...were of a generally lower order than boarders'. The day started in at least some of the houses with a period of exercise outside, regardless of the weather; in High House all members of the house did ten minutes physical jerks under the supervision of the House Seniors, and in Hyde Abbey the alternatives were 15 minutes of games practice—'I remember in my first summer term going daily into school with stinging hands because, during this period, enormous beefy girls had been hurling or bouncing cricket balls at junior girls grouped around them. It was no use trying to avoid the pain by deliberately missing the ball; they went on firing at you until you had stopped enough balls to satisfy them'—or walking round the grounds, for which it was vital to have pre-selected a companion.

Provisions for break were sent to school from each house in hampers: one house had an unvarying diet of bread and butter, and girls used to stand at break time on the edges of groups gathered around other house hampers, trying to exchange it for more delectable fare. A new housemistress immediately endeared herself by providing cream buns! At the end of the morning girls went back to their houses for lunch, and in the winter games followed. In the summer 'prep' was done in the afternoon and games played after tea. One girl remembers idyllic afternoons in the house garden doing prep on folding desks, wearing swim suits and 'garden hats, grey, such as small boys wear'. In some houses too the girls used to sleep out in the garden when the weather was good: at Hillcroft they brought back camp beds at the beginning of the summer term, and put them out on the gravel paths; the housemistress slept on the verandah.

After games, in the old boarding houses jugs of hot water would be placed in each cubicle by the maid (to whom girls were not supposed to speak) and the pupils changed into their own clothes; only three or four outfits were allowed, and there was a great scandal once when one girl was found to have 22 dresses. Evenings seem to have passed pleasantly enough; in some houses housemistresses used to read aloud, or records were played and even danced to. A certain amount of entertainment in the form of concerts, lectures, talks with slides and home-produced plays occurred: one girl remarks that entertainment was brought to them rather than them going out for it, and that when they did go out to the Guildhall for a concert or the annual performance of Gilbert and Sullivan, 'we were safely in the gallery well away from contamination'. One solitary attendance at a lecture by Sir Bernard Pares in the College in 1937 is recorded, and there was a story, probably apocryphal, current at the time that girls were instructed 'if you meet any boys of Winchester College when you are out walking, you must put on your gloves and look to the ground'.

A good deal of control in ways which would not now be acceptable was exercised by housemistresses, prefects and House Seniors. One girl remarks that the prefects seemed much more awe-inspiring and middle-aged that the younger Staff, and another remembers that in a 'gamesy' house the Head of House made them learn all the fixture lists by heart. Sweets could only be brought back at the beginning of term and half-term, and were handed in to be issued (in the case of juniors at least) only in strictly controlled quantities. Girls had to supply housemistresses with lists drawn up by their parents of the names of people to whom they might write.

Weekends appear to have been fairly uneventful: prep and mending on Saturday mornings, and there are some very happy memories of picnics; walking picnics in the winter and summer picnics in Avington Park with bully beef and ship's biscuit to eat, but there were also matches with compulsory watching for all those not taking part, remembered as 'miserable cold vigils on the sidelines' in the winter. 'Saturday evenings were times of warmth, sweets, reading, conversation, gramophones and dancing'.

Sunday mornings were occupied with church-going in crocodiles, but as one girl remarks, it was almost the only time of the week when they got outside the school grounds. A few girls could go to Matins at the Cathedral, but there seems to have been some restriction on numbers, probably dating back to the 1920s when some elderly ladies had apparently objected to the girls in the Cathedral. After that they sat on each side of William Rufus's tomb and had to stand whenever the choir did so. There was no such restriction on Cathedral Evensong, and many Old Girls have written appreciatively of the opportunity to go regularly to the Cathedral, and grow familiar with its beauty. After church an account of the sermon had to be written, and the Vicar of Holy Trinity endeared himself to the girls by slipping his sermon notes to the Head Girl on the way out.

Sunday summer dresses come in for some comment; at first they were tailored natural coloured tussore with long sleeves, and with them were worn cream-coloured lisle stockings and brown lace up shoes with a panama hat. Later the dresses were changed for a floral design and the hats for chip-straw. In the winter evidently velveteen dresses were fashionable, and one Old Girl remembers eating a 'splendid high tea' of soup, bread, dripping and raw onions, which they ate on their laps wearing science overalls over their velveteen dresses. Afterwards they sang hymns. 'Space in the drawing room was limited, so the three smallest sat on top of the piano, keeping the pages down with their feet'. In some houses the girls were expected to go for a walk on Sunday afternoon in addition to their walk to church, and great was the relief when this custom was discontinued and they were allowed to lie on their beds and read. There are also pleasant memories of long summer afternoons out in the grounds, lying in the sun and reading, and, after the new boarding houses were built, of being able to use the swimming pool and tennis courts.

Although a tremendous programme of rebuilding had been undertaken and completed in the early 1930s the school was still not really adequately housed. A clear trend in favour of boarding emerged during these years, and as soon as the economic situation eased somewhat, Miss Finlay found that her available boarding places were oversubscribed. Indeed, with numbers running at about 312 the whole school felt too full: the new teaching block had been designed to house between 275 and 300 pupils. In 1935 the Council took the view that numbers should be kept down to 300, but with the heavy financial commitments now resting on them, the extra fees were very desirable, and in 1936 Palm Hall on St Giles Hill was leased as a 'waiting' house. During 1937 and 1938 the situation became more complicated: numbers of day girls continued to decline, and could not be made up by taking more boarders, and once this started to happen the school began to have difficulty in covering its loan interest and repayments. In 1937 numbers hovered around the 300 mark and the school broke about even: by the end of 1938 numbers had sunk to below 290 and the bank overdraft had increased. It was clear that more boarding accommodation was vitally necessary, but the school could not possibly embark on the building of another double boarding house. As a temporary expedient, St Giles Mount was leased for six months to deal with the immediate overflow.

By this time other problems were emerging, not of the school's own making. In 1933 Hitler had turned Germany into a one-party state, and two years later Germany denounced the Treaty of Versailles and started re-arming. The first sign in the school records of the anxiety which was beginning to be felt throughout Europe is found in Miss Finlay's Report to the Council of March 1936, when she wrote 'National events threw everything else into the background during the first week of term'. At this time Britain was just collecting itself after the abdication of Edward VIII, Italy had just attacked Abyssinia, the Spanish Civil War was looming, and Hitler was preparing for the first of his territorial seizures with the occupation of the Rhineland.

At the beginning of 1938 the County Air Raids Precaution Officer visited the school twice, to discuss its protection in time of war, and to arrange for a demonstration on how to deal with incendiary bombs. Enquiries had also been made by the authorities about the sanatorium and its equipment. After the Nazi occupation of Austria in March 1938, St Swithun's received an enquiry from a school in London, asking whether in event of war some of their girls could be taken in. The Munich crisis of September 1938 caused a rather anxious beginning to the new school year, and during that term the school got its first air raid trenches, partly dug by the Staff. Senior girls helped to assemble gas masks for the city of Winchester. Staff also began to attend Air Raid Precaution (A.R.P.) lectures, and one old girl remembers that the housekeeper and the senior girls were left in charge of Earlsdown while the housemistress and her assistant both went to these lectures. Over 100 senior girls started taking first aid classes.

Despite the threatening situation, the Council clearly did not yet regard war as inevitable, for in December 1938 they were considering plans and prices for a second boarding house. When, at the beginning of 1939, it was decided that the air raid trenches were too far from the school building to be satisfactory, plans were made for the new trenches to be linked with a proposed underground corridor in the new boarding house. Two concrete trenches were finally provided, at the back of Hyde Abbey, parallel with the line of trees at the back of the main building, one capable of holding 150 people, the other 200. On Parents Day 1939 Miss Finlay invited inspection of them.

It was not until July 1939 that it was finally decided to postpone the new building, and by that time Miss Finlay was reporting to Council that the international situation was having some effect on numbers. 'A quiet period brings many parents, but alarms and excursions bring a cessation or change of plan such as delay in entry or withdrawal'. The general view at that time was that the school was in a relatively 'safe' area, and that it was well provided with air raid precautions. Inquiries were received about possible accommodation in the case of evacuation from schools in London, Portsmouth and Southampton. In an interesting comment on how the situation was affecting schools generally, Miss Finlay said that some schools were lowering fees to attract more pupils, and that some parents had withdrawn children from St Swithun's, saying that they had been offered fees elsewhere which they were not in a position to refuse.

September 1939 saw the entry of Great Britain into the Second World War, and also saw a worsening of the financial position of St Swithun's. The permitted bank overdraft had now been exceeded by £2,000, and the Council was committed to the installation of a new central heating system, a decision taken in July 1939 and estimated to cost £2,300. Economies were made by not replacing some teaching staff, dispensing with a gardener, and cutting the library grant, and it was decided to discontinue the mortgage repayment for the time being. Despite these moves, the situation was still serious.

The immediate impact of the war on the school was in detail rather than in major respects. For two terms St Swithun's allowed the Atherley School, evacuated from Southampton, to use its buildings during the afternoon, and most school activities in the main building had to be completed during daylight hours, because of the blackout requirements. Trench and fire practices took place weekly, and the sick room and offices in the main school were sandbagged as First Aid posts. Numbers in the school were down to 280, and because of Service postings it was thought that day girl numbers might fluctuate considerably. The school had been due to have a general inspection, but it was decided to ask that this might be postponed because of the unusual situation. This was agreed, but early in 1940 it was reinstated by the Board of Education, as part of a general policy to inspect all schools in the area which had not been evacuated. It took place in May during a week in which the school for the first time spent part of a night in the trenches, sharing them with some of the Inspectors!

With the German offensive against Belgium and Holland on 10 May 1940, the situation changed very quickly. On 23 May the Emergency Committee—created to carry on school business in case it should be difficult to convene full Council meetings in war time—heard that seven of the school's men (presumably ground and maintenance staff) would join the Local Defence Volunteers with a view to protecting the school from the possible danger of enemy parachutists. There is a fascinating reference by Miss Finlay to this episode in her testimonial in the 1946 *Chronicle* to Mr. and Mrs. Lawrence, the school's caretaker and cook respectively. She wrote 'When war came, she [Mrs. Lawrence] helped us turn the waiting room into a guard room ordered by military authority where I gave out arms and she supplied cocoa to the men...'. What a picture that conjures up!

At the same meeting on 23 May, Miss Finlay asked whether the Committee would consider the question of evacuation should this become essential. It was felt, however, that the time had not yet come to discuss the possibility, and that when and if the need arose, orders would probably be received from the government. Four days later (27 May) the evacuation of the British Expeditionary Force from France was ordered, and the next day the Belgians surrendered to the Germans. A special meeting of the School Council took place on 7 June primarily to meet two of the Inspectors who had been at the school the previous month, and at that meeting Miss Finlay drew the Council's attention to three questions which many parents were asking: whether they might have their children home if need should arise; whether the school might move to another area; and whether the school was taking any other steps, such as participating in the Overseas Scheme for sending children to other countries in the Empire for safety. She was instructed by the Council to reply that the school was not at the moment contemplating moving, but that in accordance with the Board of Education's wishes, parents should feel free to take their children away if they wished.

By this time the evacuation of troops from Dunkirk had taken place. Britain now faced a previously unimaginable situation—that Hitler might well overrun the whole of France, and that all Britain had to defend itself from a German invasion was such men and equipment as had been recovered from France, together with such reserves as had been held in this country, and the help of the civilian population. It seemed quite possible that any normal life such as would include the continuation of regular schooling might soon come to an end, and it was also recognised that Britain would soon be the target of widespread and heavy aerial bombardment. It is in this emotionally heightened and unnatural atmosphere that the subsequent actions of both Council and Headmistress must be considered.

Between the Council meeting of 7 June, and a meeting of the Finance Committee on 21 June (two days before the surrender of France) 27 boarders and nine day girls had already been withdrawn or were planning to leave. At the meeting of the Finance Committee a decision was taken to end the summer term early on 1 July, and notices to this effect were sent out to parents. By that date the number of those leaving rose to more than seventy. When the full Council met again (on 26 June), this action was questioned, and Miss Finlay was asked to explain why the Finance Committee had taken it. It was felt by some members of Council that the act was unconstitutional, and that it would set a bad example to other schools in the area, particularly to those evacuated from Portsmouth.

Miss Finlay informed the Council that the boarding houses had already been inspected by Ministry of Health officials, with a view to their being taken over by the government as hospital annexes should the need arise. It was also believed that the Winchester district might be designated as an evacuation area, in which case there would be only 48 hours for the school to leave, and no public assistance for obtaining the necessary transport would be provided. The possibility of invasion had also to be faced, and, as one member of Council pointed out, that risk was a totally different consideration for a girls' school than in the case of the opposite sex.

Exception was taken to the fact that Miss Finlay had acquired some of her information in a private interview with the authorities and had thus acted outside her powers; in reply she stated that she realised she might get into trouble, but was ready to offer her resignation at any time. However, when the Council was asked to approve the action taken by the Finance Committee, it did so, by 11 votes to three, and several members spoke strongly in support of Miss Finlay's actions. It was agreed that the school should be kept open after 1 July for any day girls who wished to complete the normal term. Miss Finlay was also concerned to make provision for examination candidates, so that they could enjoy some peace and quiet in which to take their School Certificate examinations in July, and it was agreed that she, and some of the Staff, should go with the candidates to stay in Oxford at Miss Finlay's old college of St Hilda's, and that Miss Clark should stay in Winchester as acting Headmistress to keep the school going for the day girls.

On the day Miss Finlay left for Oxford two officers representing the Major-General of Defence visited the school in the evening, in the belief that it had already been evacuated and was standing empty. When they discovered this was not so they still asked to be shown round, and were heard to remark that it would make an ideal H.Q. building. The Chairman was naturally told about this at once, and an Emergency Committee meeting was summoned to consider a new situation—should the school try to remain where it was or move to other premises? Up to this point it does not seem that voluntary evacuation had been seriously considered: when it came up during the meeting of 26 June the point had not been pursued. The Treasurer now raised a further point for consideration. The bank overdraft was running at £5,500 above its permitted level, and the school simply could not afford to maintain its present buildings if its numbers were going to be permanently reduced.

In a series of meetings throughout July (Miss Finlay being absent in Oxford throughout) the discussion went on. Letters were sent to parents to try to find out their future intentions; it was suggested that the school might be divided between Oxford and Winchester with staff commuting between the two. An attempt to find totally new accommodation revealed that most suitable premises in 'safe' areas had already been taken by schools which had taken the decision to move much earlier. Above all, it was recognised that to move would cost money which the school could ill-afford. Thoughts therefore turned towards the possibility of letting the main school buildings to the military authorities, and concentrating the remaining boarders and the teaching in the houses on St Giles Hill, renting any other houses in the area which might be suitable. Towards the end of July the decision to follow this course of action was taken, and it was announced that the school would re-open on 11 September. Some of the Staff would not be required because of the smaller number of pupils, and although they could not be given proper notice their salaries were paid up to Christmas.

It is difficult to discover what Miss Finlay's feelings about all this were. She had in any case been due to retire in 1940 (at the age of 58) but after the outbreak of war she agreed to continue to serve for another two years or until the end of the war, whichever proved the shorter. Now, however, with all the anxieties and problems which had developed, she felt she could not go on, and wrote to the Chairman from Oxford to say that she wished to resign at Christmas 1940. She did not return to Winchester at the end of term, and was felt by the Council to be in a condition of some strain. A small committee was therefore appointed to confer with Miss Clark and other staff about the arrangements for the Autumn Term; it was decided that the girls should return one week earlier, on 18 September. Provision was also made for the renting of two extra houses, Chilcomb Rectory and Hillbrow, with the possibility of a third, the Gaer, if the number of girls returning warranted it.

During August the Council continued to meet in conjunction with Miss Clark, who was responsible for staffing arrangements, and the allocation of houses for boarding and teaching was made. Staff who had received notice at the end of the Summer Term were invited to return unless they had already made other arrangements—teaching posts were evidently very difficult to obtain at this moment—and it was decided to concentrate the teaching in LeRoy and the newly rented Chilcomb Rectory. The boarders were divided among the remaining houses: High House and Hillcroft divided between Hillcroft itself and St Giles Mount which adjoined it; Hyde and Palm Hall in Palm Hall and Hillbrow; Earlsdown in the Gaer; and LeRoy in Earlsdown. Staff were asked to come back to help with the move, as at some point not now recorded the main school buildings had been taken over at a week's notice by the Royal Army Medical Corps, the school retaining use of the playing fields, swimming bath, sanatorium and one laboratory. The various buildings on St Giles Hill were considered sufficient for 175 girls, and it was agreed that numbers should be kept to this total from the beginning of 1941, in the proportion of 110 boarders to 65 day girls.

Public announcement of Miss Finlay's impending retirement was not made until after the beginning of the autumn term of 1940, and in the interim the Council had decided that in order to give themselves time to advertise and to select a new Headmistress properly they would appoint Miss Clark as Acting Headmistress for the spring term of 1941, with the new Head taking office in May 1941.

Thus it was that Miss Finlay's last term was not altogether the happy, easy one which a long-serving and highly successful Headmistress deserved. There were many adjustments to be made to the new and somewhat cramped conditions in which the school was to exist during the war; provision had to be made for safety during air raid alerts, and bunks provided for sleeping downstairs if necessary. There were difficulties with heating and hot water, and perhaps most disturbing of all, there was no one room large enough for the whole school to meet together, although this difficulty was somewhat mitigated by the kind offices of the vicar of All Saints, who put his church at the school's disposal. Farewells to Miss Finlay were also somewhat subdued—she went to a party at each house in turn—and because of war time restrictions on printing no full tribute could be paid to her in the *Chronicle*, which was not published at all in 1940 and only in a very limited form in 1941. A presentation to her at the Old Girls meeting is recorded, and a speech made by Prunella Bodington, thanking Miss Finlay for all she had done for the Old Girls Association.

> Those of us who are of Miss Finlay's generation in the School owe her even more; we have never known the School without her and shall always regard her as inseparable from it in the memories of our days here. My first recollections of Miss Finlay as a person—as distinct from someone who appeared automatically on the platform and was greeted in a chorus of four words—dates from my first week in the School and my firm attachment to a girl who wore gaiters! These, I remember, seemed to necessitate us both being involved in the fearful predicament of being 'locked in' at the end of almost every morning. I, whose sin was so obviously the greater, since I did not even possess the gaiters, was eventually seized by an irate prefect and thrust unceremoniously across the threshold of Miss Finlay's room—thus to make her acquaintance for the first time. Since those distant days we have all crossed this threshold many times with diminished trepidation and increasing pleasure and have many other memories which stand out just as clearly; of Study Circles, of Miss Finlay's end-of-term talks and of coming back to our first Old Girls' weekend and of Miss Finlay revealing to us that quality which we had always known she possessed, of making each one of us feel ourself to be the *one* person she wanted to see.

To some of her Old Girls she was known as 'Fin' and one writing of her time at the school says 'I still cherish certain memories, Fin and Miss Pinchard making their majestic way down the main drive. That duo out-did any actress's arrival on stage...The deafening clatter, in the silence of the School assembled for Prayers, of Miss Pinchard's rings being deposited on the top of that superb piano...Fin's extraordinary ability to fidget her Edwardian hair-do backwards and forwards in the most amazing way'. This same movement is recalled by another, who used to play Miss Finlay's own piano to her: 'every time the slightest mishap occurred you could *feel* her eyebrows being raised while her hair seemed to be lowered (a very characteristic gesture of reproof)'.

Despite her small size she had great presence and composure 'almost like a nun' said one Old Girl recently. When Prunella Bodington gave the address at her memorial service in 1978, she not only recalled this poise and good carriage but also her beautiful voice, 'light and clear', and 'the concentration and dedication with which she read, prayed and spoke. It has always seemed to me that there was something about Miss Finlay's presence and her voice which commanded—no, I would say "drew like a magnet", the attention and concentration of her listeners. Otherwise how would I remember across 60 years the exact intonation of her voice as she introduced the Second Prayer..."Ask and it shall be given you, seek and ye shall find, knock and it shall be opened unto you; for everyone that asketh receiveth, he that seeketh findeth and to him that knocketh it shall be opened". These words to me reflected Miss Finlay's deep faith, her strong conviction and dedication to the Christian way of life...which was perhaps her most outstanding quality'.

After her retirement these Christian qualities were put to full use. At first, to her evident embarrassment, owing to war time housing difficulties, she had to go on living in Winchester—'I live there as an invisible friend'she said—but she then went to live in London, to immerse herself in a great deal of church work and in an immense correspondence with, and interest in, Old Girls, which lasted until the end of her long life. At the age of 90 she came down to the opening of Finlay House in 1972, and when it was suggested that she might like to speak sitting down said firmly 'I always stand to speak, one's thoughts are not so clear lolling in a chair'. It was at this time that she made a tape of her recollections which has been of great value in compiling this history.

IV

Miss Watt, 1941-1952

For the Spring Term of 1941 Miss Clark was in charge of the School as Acting Headmistress, but Miss Finlay's successor had already been appointed before Christmas 1940, and came to the school in May 1941. She was Miss Grace Watt, another historian, from Cambridge. She had been Headmistress of Portsmouth High School G.P.D.S.T. for nine years before coming to Winchester, and had previously taught history at Cheltenham and St Paul's Girls' School, where she had been highly regarded both for her teaching ability and her intellectual capacity.

She came to St Swithun's at a difficult time, the school was diminished and crowded in its remaining buildings and not yet really settled into a routine, and the War was at an unhappy stage: shipping losses were at their height, the German armies had come into the Mediterranean area with devastating effect, and the civilian population had had an uncomfortable winter with London carrying the heavy burden of the Blitz and its losses in life and buildings. Staff remember the difficulty of finding accommodation in Winchester swollen with evacuees, and of feeding themselves with little time to queue for food which, though always available, often took a long time to buy. They also had to carry much of the responsibility for firewatching on the hilltop initially, then some help became available and the members of staff living in or near school houses were divided into three shifts and were 'on patrol' once in three weeks; the school 'men' also took their turn. From 1942 the school undertook the firewatching for two nights a week and the City authorities were responsible for the other five, the school providing beds and warmth for the firewatchers. This was quite enough as classes had to be taught after sleepless nights—alerts were fairly frequent though there were only two occasions during the whole war when bombs were dropped—and in some cases the staff found themselves lighting the fires in classrooms before morning school began. In the summer when fireplaces were not in use for their normal purposes a few more pupils could be fitted in as the staff could stand in the fireplace to teach! 'Gym in the old Earlsdown laundry was quite a feat, but happily no-one fell into the tubs, knocked out any one's eye or vaulted onto the stove'.

One member of the staff who was at St Swithun's throughout the War thought that the girls probably found it more difficult than was realised at the time to adapt to the cramped conditions and particularly to the 'doubling up' of Houses, each of which had strong loyalties and individual traditions. For some, however, the St Giles Hill houses had a more homely atmosphere. One Old Girl writing of her experience at school during the War, says 'I was in Hillcroft during the war years when conditions were spartan, by today's standards quite ghastly; but we all survived and I am quite sure it did me no harm whatever and probably much good, as I am very immune to all the common ailments!'

'All fuels were desperately short, more and more economies had to be made as the war progressed. Our bedrooms had no heating whatever and during cold spells it was not unknown for those sleeping on the top floor to wake in the morning and find a sheet of ice on top of our jug of water—we all had a jug and basin on a washstand near our bed.

Evenings and bedtime were not better, as the poor old boiler gave up providing hot water after two or three girls had taken a bath, even though we had a mark on the bath five inches from the bottom to limit the depth of water. If you were number six on the rota, a bath was an extremely chilly experience, but we always filled our hot water bottles with the tepid liquid. During the bombing of Southampton, we all had to sleep downstairs in a corridor on bunks and I had the dubious pleasure of sharing mine with the Housemistress's golden retriever who used it during the day—she was elderly and distinctly smelly.

The common room fire was a small hearth, made even smaller by the addition of bricks on each side, but the flames did allow us to make some home-made toffee if we could spare some sugar from our weekly allowance (was it 2 oz?), which was kept in the dining room in a labelled screw-topped jar. A small pile of sugar was put onto a piece of paper and the poker heated to red hot. By skilfully touching the sugar it could produce a lump of brown substance resembling toffee, but frequently it would change into a charred, horrid-tasting mess and probably set light to the paper as well. I can never remember anyone forbidding this dangerous practice.

Another dangerous job we all had to do was to walk around the outside of the house to check there were no chinks of light showing through the blackout. It was always pitch dark and the gardens were very rough due to minimum maintenance. I walked into a wall on one night and I didn't realise anything was wrong until I felt blood pouring down my cheek, the intense cold had numbed my head, but I have the scar to this day.'

Another remembrance of war-time feeding was of much pumpkin pie and peanut butter, which produced life-long abhorrence of both. As a first economy move the school clothing list was reduced to 36 items but by the end of the war the only articles of uniform clothing being universally worn were a school coat and hat, and a store of second-hand clothing had been started. An appeal for old lacrosse sticks was sent out through the *Chronicle* newsheet, and it was also reported that tennis was somewhat restricted because of a shortage of balls.

Because of travel difficulties and petrol rationing, very few outside matches were played during the whole period of the war, and outside entertainments also almost ceased. An exception to this was the splendid series of concerts held in the Guildhall, which in normal times would probably have taken place in Southampton. A tremendous appetite for good music developed during the war and they were always packed. On the other hand, school societies and clubs flourished; they had always been a strong feature of St Swithun's life but between the wars their fortunes had fluctuated depending on the enthusiasm of girls and, to a certain extent, on the energy and popularity of individual staff, though they were always run by a committee of girls with staff attending as representatives rather than actually holding executive office.

Amongst the most popular of the clubs and societies were the Dramatic Society and the Music Club, the Debating Society, the Historical Society, the Science Society and two new ones created during the war, the Cercle Français and the Geography Lodge whose main interest was to hear talks on and look at pictures of foreign travel at a time when any travel abroad was impossible and even in the British Isles was difficult. During the war, for the first time, the College lent their Music School for two school concerts, and another one was given in the Town Hall. As the petrol situation eased a little in 1946 a few school expeditions became possible again, and there was much pleasure and excitement for a generation starved of 'outings'. The Historical Society visited Southampton to see what was left of the old town after the bombing, and the Cercle Français went to London to see *Phedre* by the Comedie Française.

The school's contributions to the war effort also occupied quite a lot of time. Almost everyone in the school joined the War Savings group and contributed a regular amount each week, amounting in all the war years to over £1,300. Special efforts to collect money in 'Warship' week, 'Aid to Russia' week, 'Wings for Victory' week and many others, involved the school in entertainments at which entry was paid for in National Savings stamps, in drawing outlines of submarines on the pavement to be covered by pennies from passers-by and in supervising a mile of pennies along the streets of Winchester. All through the War, too, everyone knitted scarves, socks, balaclava helmets, operation stockings and pullovers for the Forces, and the U.G.S. mission, undergoing much hardship through bombing in Camberwell, was not forgotten. Early on in the War a mine-sweeper, the H.M.S. *Filey Bay*, was adopted by the school, and towards the end of the War a naval officer came from Portsmouth to talk to the school about the work of minesweepers and to answer such questions as he judged would not involve state secrets. Regular help was given by some of the senior girls at a War Nursery established in Winchester, and under Miss Snowball's supervision they helped to grow vegetables, and in some cases went to farming camps in the school holidays.

So in many ways, school life was more diversified and less restricted during the war, but the main purpose of the school, 'sound learning', was always kept in sight. Throughout the war St Swithun's girls continued to gain entrance to Universities whether they took up their places immediately or deferred their entry in order to go straight into some form of war work. A glance through the news of Old Girls in the 1943 *Chronicle* newsheet reveals the following interesting variety of war-time occupations and news: Engineer; Technical Flight Sergeant in the W.A.A.F.; Mobile V.A.D.; Hospital Cook; Coder in the W.R.N.S.; a mere wartime housewife looking after her three-year old daughter, helping to look after invalid father-in-law and typing weekly restricted letters to husband interned in Singapore; a W.R.N.S. dispatch rider attached to Staff of C.-in-C. Portsmouth; a Land Girl; Leading Firewoman and instructress, fire station, Winchester; one Old Girl writes that she is engaged on confidential Government war work of a Mobile nature; another that she is serving with the American Ambulance Great Britain and reading for her Bar Finals; another is working for the Hampshire War Agricultural Committee issuing rations for pigs, poultry, goats and cows; and yet another has escaped from Singapore with her two children and is now a Captain in the R.A.M.C. in a hospital in N.W. India: her husband is posted missing, presumed killed, in Singapore.

Paradoxically as the war went on, so more girls tended to stay on into the VI form; although liable to be called up at 18, and able to volunteer for various kinds of war work at 17, they sometimes found it difficult to be accepted at that age, and after Miss Watt had organised some secretarial training for the VI form they found that their chances of an interesting wartime occupation was increased by the extra training and time at school. The school was also able, on Miss Watt's initiative, to provide, in two of the house kitchens, the first Domestic Science teaching in its history. She considered this an important extension of VI form opportunities for the less academic girls.

Adjusting the school curriculum and timetable to wartime needs was only one of the many demands made on Miss Watt on her arrival at St Swithun's. The already difficult financial situation of the school had been exacerbated by the events of the summer of 1940. It was estimated that the reduced numbers in the school cost it £4,000 in lost fees though it saved some £1,600 in running costs. At first no rent was received for the requisitioned main school, and until this was agreed with the War Office at £2,000 per annum, the school found difficulty in meeting even its day-to-day running costs. In these circumstances, all the Staff agreed to take a 5 per cent cut in their salary and the Council pledged itself to restore full salaries as soon as possible. This was done early in 1942 but all through the war the school was extremely short of money and with rising costs the Council felt justified in announcing its first rise in fees since 1930; they went up by £3 a term for boarders in May 1942.

Once some kind of equilibrium had been restored two very valuable and longserving members of the Council felt that the time had come to give up office, Dr. Davies retired from the Chairmanship of the Council, an office he had held since 1927, and Mr. Madams, having negotiated a very favourable working agreement with the school's bank, felt that he must give up the Treasurership after 19 years. Between them, these two had seen the school through two moves—from North Walls and now from its new buildings—and had guided it through the financial hazards of the building programme of the 1930s. Finally they had settled it down again after the uncertainties of the summer of 1940: they deserved to be relieved of some of their burden. Canon Spencer Leeson, the Headmaster of Winchester College, became the new Chairman, and Mr. Madams was succeeded by Mr. Austin. As final evidence that the school was once more secure and thriving it was decided to hold a proper Speech Day in June 1942 in the Guildhall. The speaker on that occasion was the President of the Board of Education, R. A. Butler who, two years later, was to be the author of the important Education Act restructuring England's state school system and he spoke specifically on this occasion of the enquiry which he had just instituted into the association of the Public Schools with the general system of education. This was one of the few occasions during the war when all the school could be together, but that summer gave another opportunity of a less formal nature; St Swithun's Day was fine so the whole school met for prayers in the garden of Chilcomb and afterwards Miss Clark told something of the history of the school since its foundation.

During 1942 the R.A.M.C. took over the whole of the school's new buildings, thereby depriving them of the only laboratory left to them, and necessitating the hasty removal of furniture which had been stacked into two empty rooms. Later in the year the whole building was handed over to the American Army as a military hospital. A description of the school, first as a British and then as an American hospital, is given in an article contributed to the 1945 *Chronicle* by A. F.: 'One day in July 1940, the last of a succession of cars rattled sadly down the drive, bearing away into exile the last member of St Swithun's Staff.

'For some weeks the buildings stood empty, but in August the advance-party of the British Army took possession, creating first havoc, then a hospital. The hospital staff followed, taking up their quarters in the Boarding-house Wing, and, finally, came the patients. The School now assumed a purely medical aspect. The Form-rooms became wards, the Domestic-Science Kitchen was used for blood-transfusion, the Physics Laboratory and Cloak-room (with dividing wall removed) became the operating theatre. Bramston Hall became a resuscitation ward, and the Biology Laboratory a ward for broken limbs.

'By the summer of 1942, however, the Americans were well into the war and the British Army sub-let the building to the American Medical Corps. Now the School grounds were invaded by hordes of our Allies, who made huts on the lawns and holes in the walls. Sinks were fixed, pulleys hung, a lift was improvised outside the Kitchen window. Every available inch of space was filled by a bed, except for the Boarding-house Kitchens, which, having been prepared with barred windows for cases of psycho-neurosis (an euphemism for lunacy), were fortunately never needed. Thus the building was transformed into a true American hospital.

'Into the midst of this grim and urgent activity was thrown a ray of gaiety—Romance! A wedding between two members of the hospital staff took place in the Hall. It was a real, genuine wedding, with all the traditional trappings of white dresses, bridesmaids and orange blossom. Other diversions from the constant struggle against sickness were the frequent E.N.S.A. and U.S.O. shows, which brought down British and American actors and even film stars to entertain the staff and patients.'

'Now the school had use only of the playing fields and even those were on occasion invaded by military vehicles and equipment, involving Miss Watt in much correspondence with the officers in charge. Members of the school remember going to the swimming pool in a strict crocodile under military escort, past sunbathing convalescent troops, and being told in no circumstances either to look at them or peer in at the windows. The G.I.s were also apparently very intrigued and mystified by cricket. 'When they asked to handle a ball and felt its hardness they could not get over the fact that everyone except the wicket keeper fielded such a hard ball with bare hands'.

The strains on Miss Watt must have been considerable and it clearly had not been appreciated when she was appointed that she suffered from a degree of deafness. It is unfortunate that this combined with her other anxieties and made her difficult to communicate with on occasions, and also led to misunderstandings with parents, staff and Council, with the result that in 1943 a number of Council members resigned, and staff resignations, particularly among senior members of the staff, were higher than they might otherwise have been. Her undoubted gifts as an educationalist could only have limited scope during wartime and this must hve increased a sense of frustration. Nevertheless, she was able, in 1942, with the encouragement of the Council, to estabish a Parent-Teacher Association which has been flourishing ever since, and in the next year she instituted a School Committee consisting of two representatives of each form from LIV upwards, together with Staff representatives, under her Chairmanship.

Another innovation was the 'Free Study Week' during which all periods except the last one each morning were used by the girls to work at assignments in their various subjects in special rooms, supervised by subject staff. Each girl had to cover either a major or a minor assignment in each subject. Miss Watt reported to the Council that it had been considered a great success by staff and girls and the experiment was repeated in succeeding years. All these developments, though excellent in themselves, meant that more was being asked of the staff in already difficult circumstances, and this contributed to a sense of strain which began to be felt in 1943. The war was at last going better, but the Council noted that staff absences because of illness were increasing.

In the spring of 1943, too, Winchester had the more serious of its two bomb incidents. One morning in March a solitary German aircraft dropped a stick of bombs on the Hyde area of the city causing a number of casualties. On St Giles Hill the incident was clearly visible just before morning school was to begin. When the school bus coming up from the city became late, concern spread among the staff; relief when it did arrive was tempered by the sight of white faces amongst the passengers. It transpired that the bus had just moved away from the traffic lights on the corner of Jewry Street and North Walls when a bomb fell very close to where it had been waiting for the lights to turn green.

As the war went on, Winchester became steadily more crowded with troops and during 1943 more and more of these were Americans, many of them coloured. One day, one of them called at one of the school houses with a string bag full of oranges and candies saying that he thought perhaps the children didn't have too many of them.

The School's Diamond Jubilee fell in 1944 and tentative plans for its celebration had been discussed during the preceding year, coupled with the launching of an Appeal for the school's immediate needs. But in the event, the celebration had to be postponed. In the spring of 1944, Winchester, together with many other coastal regions in the south and south east of England became a 'prohibited area' which meant that no one could visit it without a special permit, and on the by-pass below Spitfire Bridge a solid line of all sorts of military vehicles covered with camouflage tarpaulins was parked facing Southampton. It did not require a great deal of imagination to realise that all this was connected with the expected invasion of France. On the last day of the Spring term the seniors were all called together by Miss Watt and told that when they got home they must be discreet about the military preparations they had seen during the term. A member of staff present said that all felt the solemnity and momentousness of the occasion and that it was very sobering.

When the school came back in early May, the vehicles were still there, and on one occasion the sound of a convoy of heavy tanks going through the town by North Walls and Bar End rose up to Morn Hill causing momentary alarm, so menacing was it. Then on the night of 5-6 June the noise became continuous as endless streams of planes and gliders passed over carrying the first invasion troops, and next morning a member of staff going to teach the Upper V in their south-facing classroom was greeted by a row of backs as the whole class was standing on its desks looking towards the sea and France, where by now they knew the action was taking place. The excitement and optimism engendered by the successful establishment of a bridgehead in France received a check, when very shortly the first flying bombs of 'doodle-bugs' began to cross the south coast, and School Certificate that year was taken while they were still active. In the middle of one exam a doodle-bug was heard; everyone had to take cover on the ground floor, forbidden to talk of their papers, until the danger was passed and they could go back to their exam. A member of staff who was invigilating commented 'It seemed a long time to keep up a non-conversation'.

With the invasion came a rush of activity in the hospital in the main buildings: mattresses had been put down in all the main corridors and in the first few days after the invasion long lines of ambulances moved slowly up to the front door depositing there the first wounded. These included German troops, brought back from France, before they could be sent to more permanent hospitals; as many as 700 patients arrived in a single day. This rush continued until August, and then gradually both patients and staff were transferred to other hospitals. By the time the school returned in September the buildings were empty. The Board of Education had already agreed that the return of school buildings was a matter of urgency but told the Council that it would have to conduct its own negotiations for their release. This inevitably led to delays. Although by October it was known that the school would be de-requisitioned shortly, the actual order was not received until February 1945. Miss Watt had already made a partial inspection of the buildings in October and thought then that the school could not hope to return to them before the summer term of 1945.

It was understood that the War Office would eventually pay for the dilapidations, but the school would have to pay the initial cost of getting the buildings into working order. At that time no building work costing more than £100 could be undertaken without a licence. The date of de-requisition, 26 February 1945, came, and no licence had been received for the additional £700 necessary, so Miss Watt used some of her precious petrol ration to drive to Reading and extract the vital licence from the authorities. Then started a period of furious activity involving at first only the buildings, but later school staff, academic and domestic, and the girls themselves, as Miss Watt had started taking more entries for the summer term to begin to bring the school back to its pre-war size. One member of staff remembers that the flood of entrants were dealt with not by the ordinary entrance examination—the quantity of papers wold have been too many to cope with—but by a single essay question. As a result, 59 new girls were taken in at the beginning of the summer term. A description of the move extending over the Easter holidays was given in the *Chronicle* of 1945.

'Our move from the war-time School buildings back to the real School began on Monday, 9th April, but already on the day following the end of term, many of the Staff and a few girls tied up parcels of books and cleaned rooms, all in preparation. Miss Pym was champion in book-tying! Monday morning arrived almost simultaneously with the removers, who ranged from George, old and looking as if he suffered from rheumatism (indeed, he often remarked "Its me knees") to Ginger, a carrot-headed boy, full of vim, who, on being asked to move a certain crate, remarked, "My name's Simpson, not Samson"!'

The most amusing incident of the day was a 'chain' of books from the extreme top of the house down to the front hall, when each 'link' had to use its full strength to maintain the steady rhythm and avoid being snowed under by three or four bundles of books. We none of us can forget Mrs. Lawrence, who always came to our rescue at about 11.30 a.m. with welcome cups of tea and biscuits. The van did several trips a day from each building. We welcomed the joy-ride to and fro, to form chains at either end. The journey there was always made sitting on books and other very sharp articles; whereas, coming back, we were seated on the comparatively comfortable wooden floor. At one point we were interrupted by a ring at the door, to be met by a small boy who announced that he had heard we were now taking boys and would we accept him? We rather wished we could have done so!

The girls helped in relays, only during the first and last week of the holidays, but many of the Staff worked valiantly right through, with only a week's break before the almost equally hectic few days preceding the beginning of term. Miss Gaukroger, we fear, had even less respite than that. Four days before this date, the school and boarding-houses looked as if they would never be ready for the general return, but as the result of very hard work on the part of both teaching and domestic staff, a remarkable transformation was wrought in those few days. When V.E. Day came, with the holidays involved for the workmen, we began to wonder if the work would ever be accomplished. Most of the staff had a break for the celebrations on the Tuesday afternoon, and in the

evening many of us watched a huge bonfire blazing on St Giles' Hill, just outside our
wartime buildings. After dark, Miss Hoskyns and Miss Macpherson turned on the lights
in all the cubicles of High House and Hyde, so that the wing was a flood of light to be
seen for miles.

When we approached our finishing touches a shortage of furniture, such as tables and
armchairs, throughout the school, made everyone anxious to hold on to what she had,
and often resulted in minor disputes. Soon, however, the building was beginning to take
the shape of its former self, and we sighed with relief, knowing that we had wrought
some sort of order out of chaos. In recalling these few days, we must always remember
the wonderful work done by Mr. and Mrs. Lawrence and their band of cleaners
throughout the buildings. Had it not been for them, the school could not have stood
bright and shining to greet us on the first day of the summer term, 11 May 1945.

The concluding paragraph of Miss Watt's termly report to the Council, 25 May 1945
read 'I cannot close the report without reference to the removal which occupied most
of the holidays. Staff and girls gave splendid help, without which the work could not
possibly have been carried out in time, owing to the shortage of labour. Not only all
the school books but all the library books were tied in bundles which were passed by a
chain of girls and mistresses down to the vans and then passed up to the library and
form-rooms on arrival. Every piece of furniture was labelled, and all desks were
marked with corridor and room, a great saving of time and confusion. The situation
was highly critical, as the permit from the Ministry of Works was endlessly delayed,
so that painters, plumbers and carpenters began their work as the move took place,
instead of having finished the major repairs beforehand, as had been arranged. Day
girls worked for a week after term ended, and Boarders offered to return early, but
not many could be used, owing to domestic duties. So that the sorting and arranging
and even the shifting of the furniture were undertaken by the Staff, few of whom had
more than a fortnight's holiday and some less. But again, I am afraid that the real
burden and heat of the day fell on Mrs. Lawrence, who was unable to get her own flat
or her kitchen or school dining-room in any order until the end of the holidays, and
who was organising the cleaning piecemeal throughout. And yet, to give a true
picture, I must admit that we all enjoyed it, and have a deeper pride in the hard-won
order and cleanliness of the school which in the past were taken for granted.' It is
possible that some of the Staff found it rather less enjoyable. There is a recollection of
Mrs. Lawrence, the cook-housekeeper 'standing with a hoe in the middle of the front
stair-case. She was working at the mud which had congealed through the Army's
coco-matting and stuck on our polished oak stair. "I'll never get it back, Miss! I'll
never get it back!" was the cry I shall never forget, but "get it back" she did, with the
help of Mr. Lawrence'. On the actual day of the German surrender and the end of the
war in Europe, 8 May 1945, the Staff were still polishing and dusting accompanied by
a small portable 'wireless' set, in preparation for the beginning of term three days
later. 'Looking back, our welcome of peace was almost unsuitably humdrum—yet I
daresay that for many people the pattern had to be just that'. On the evening of the
9th, the day before the boarders came 'one or two of us chanced to find soldiers'
cartoons on the backs of oak doors and medical labels (of an indelicate nature) above
the doors in the top floor of High House. The sublime to the ridiculous—a rush for
sandpaper and rubbers and pots of white paint...'.

On the first day of term, still in the euphoria of the victory in Europe, a service of
Thanksgiving and re-dedication was held in Bramston Hall to which a number of Old
Girls were able to come, and then later in the term the postponed celebrations for the
Diamond Jubilee took place—a year late! Parents' Day was combined with the Jubilee

and a splendid tea was provided thanks to contributions of sugar and fats from parents. (Earlier in the war at O.G.A. meetings members were asked to bring their own eatables.)

With the move back into the main buildings came some rearrangement of the boarding houses on the hill. Hillcroft stayed in its own building with an unwonted sense of space, having said good-bye to High. For the rest, Earlsdown went into the original High House, Leroy stayed in its war-time home, the old Earlsdown, Palm Hall again became the Waiting House and Chilcomb was used as a Preparatory department. In the main building, meanwhile, traditions had to be re-established and routines worked out afresh. It is worth remembering that only a handful of the Staff—Misses Allen, Armit, Hobson, Leishman, Paterson, Pym and Snowball among them—and a few girls had any experience of working in that building and it was upon them that the whole school had to rely to get it running again. On the first day of that summer term the vast majority of the school, including the Headmistress was 'New', and all had to find their way round together. Nevertheless, an Old Girl in July 1945 who stood in the entrance hall watching the school go about its business could say 'You all look exactly the same'. The anonymous reporter in the *Chronicle* remarks '. . . which goes to show that the spirit of a fine institution is above that of the total of its members, and can withstand the effects of the shocks and strain of a world upheaval'.

With the surrender of the Japanese on 2 September 1945, following the dropping of atom bombs on Hiroshima and Nagasaki the previous month, the school could really begin to look forward when it assembled for the autumn term 1945, with its numbers back to 315, the pre-war level. Back too, came one of its pre-war problems: lack of space. It had already been agreed early in 1945 that the age range of the school should be extended downwards to include a kindergarten in response to evidence of local demand, provided the school could find room and that the department could be self-financing. So in September 1945 a kindergarten class of 28 children was added to the school, but as Miss Watt observed in her report to the Council in October 1945, this was only possible, with school numbers standing at over 300, so long as the two lowest forms could be housed in a separate building—in this case one of the Hill houses. This proved to be a not very satisfactory solution, since in 1946 and 1947 a good deal of rearrangement took place in these houses: Chilcomb St Swithun and St Giles Mount were bought by the school, but then, in order to accommodate a few more girls—so essential to the school finances—the Gaer was retained on a lease and the inhabitants of Chilcomb St Swithun moved into it in February 1948. In the meantime Kingsmead House in Kingsgate Street had been leased for one year to the Preparatory Department, including the Kindergarten, but this, too, was only a temporary expedient. In any case, parents did not like it very much; it was difficult of access and it was quite impossible to provide the children with a midday meal there. A lease of part of Holy Trinity Rectory in St Peter Street was negotiated and the Preparatory Department made its second move in September 1947: after September 1948 the school acquired the use of the whole Rectory.

Links began to be established with the rest of Europe, at first by visitors from overseas coming to the school. Of these, the first was a Dutch student, Agnes Zuur, who came as a result of the contribution the school was making to the relief of Holland after the Occupation. Miss Zuur had herself been a member of the Resistance, a courier, carrying dispatches and arms from one group to another and posing as a German filmstar making propaganda films to give herself an excuse for travelling about the country. She also spoke of the appalling conditions of increasing starvation and deportation of the boys and men to labour camps which all the Dutch had endured. A link was made with a school in Amsterdam through the International Schools organisation, and a number of girls acquired pen friends there. In the spring term of 1946 a Dutch girl of 12 came and spent a month at St Swithun's in form III: the reporter comments 'we gather that both she and Miss Hobson made some interesting experiments in language study'! Mlle. Vandel, a former member of staff who had retired just before the war, and had spent the war in France, wrote about her experiences and then came over on a visit. 'I grew potatoes, carrots, even tobacco! All these are very necessary as there is little to buy . . . I have learnt to make butter, very simple and necessary as we get none. Coffee is made of barley. Meat, once a week; and a small ration too . . . we have been warned that we can't expect much heating this winter, but we have enough wood to warm at least one room'. In the summer of 1946 it became possible again to go the continent, and some girls had their first taste of holidays abroad. The next spring Miss Watt organised the first school expedition abroad, and took a party of girls to Switzerland. The account of it in the *Chronicle* reflects the excitement of the first experience of Abroad, and also the particular obsession of the immediate post-war traveller with the abundance of glorious food to be found in Switzerland while food rationing was still in force in England.

'We had "that foreign feeling" as the boat docked. There were French gendarmes in cloaks and kepis just like the pictures in our text books.

We were in France. We slept fitfully as the train clanked and screamed on and we woke in Alsace. White oxen drew ploughs; the road ran up and down; there were no hedges but lots of little woods, and on the horizon real hills and far away the dim lines of snow mountains. At Basle we left the train and had our first Swiss breakfast of coffee, rolls and real butter with cherry jam.

How to compress Lugano into a paragraph? Eating two square meals a day with snacks of delicious cakes in between; buying films, shoes, watches, chocolates, bananas, oranges with no limit except the size of our purses; steamer trips on the lake cradled in mountains—to Morcote and a toil up the hills behind and a helter-skelter down again as the train went off without us—to Gandria, accessible only on foot or by steamer, lovely and peaceful with vine-covered terraces on the lake; up Monte Bre where a cold wind as well as a superb panorama of the Alps told us how high we were; day excursions up the valleys inland from Lugano, on one of which we met our king of lizards, brilliant green with a head of kingfisher blue; Bellini frescoes and the lovely facade of the Cathedral attributed to Bramante—a jumble of happy memories. And always blue skies, hot sun, the smell of warm earth and flowers everywhere.'

In 1949 Miss Watt and Miss Trigg took a party to the Austrian Tyrol in the summer holidays, and during the academic year, 1950-51, foreign contacts proliferated. Some girls made exchange visits, two school parties went to Austria, Miss Anderson took two girls to Spain in the Easter holidays, and to St Swithun's came two Swedish girls for a month in the summer, and two American mistresses for a day's visit. Two German headmistresses spent a considerable amount of time at the school during a fortnight's visit to Winchester.

This too was the year of the Festival of Britain, and many girls visited the South Bank exhibition designed to give some cheer and impetus to counteract the continuing hardship and shortages of the post-war period.

In 1946, for the first time, the school entered a team for the Schools Lacrosse Tournament, and, presaging many similar meetings, though not always with the same result, were beaten by Queen Anne's, Caversham, in the final, and in 1948, a tennis pair went to compete in the Schoolgirls' Queen's Club Tournament. Fencing thrived, and part of the Parents' Day display in 1950 consisted of a match between the school and the College: in 1952 a girl reached the final of the Junior Inter-Schools' Fencing competition.

A day never forgotten by those who took part was a visit by the great West Indian cricketer, Learie Constantine, in 1945. He had been Miss Snowball's coach, and she persuaded him to come and spend a day coaching the First XI and demonstrating his own skills. Bowling created a certain problem: he was told not to bowl full pace at the girls, and the help of College had to be enlisted to provide him with some pace bowling. Even if the XI found it an alarming experience, they were united in being charmed by his personality and enthusiasm.

Probably members of the Council were more acutely aware of how the post-war economy and its problems affected the school than staff and girls, who found that on the whole, opportunities to expand and diversify educational experience were increasing. Prices began to rise as controls were gradually removed, but in common with all schools, the Council was extremely reluctant to resort to increases in fees to cope with rising costs: it was simply not part of the Public School tradition. Very soon after the war they asked the architect who had prepared plans for two further boarding houses in 1938 to work out what the cost of building them now would be: the £24,000 of 1938 had risen to £36,000 but apart from anything else, it was considered very unlikely that a licence to build would be granted while building materials were so short and the first priority was to replace homes destroyed by wartime bombing. It then became evident that the school was not covering its commitments and stringent economy measures, even to the length of economising on teaching staff, were taken, and fee rises were reluctantly sanctioned. At the same time, numbers in the school were increased, both by the lease of the Gaer and by converting some of the maids' rooms in the double boarding houses, so that by the autumn term of 1951, for the first time, the school had more than 400 girls. Even so, new building could not be contemplated—an enquiry into the cost of new boarding houses in 1950 revealed that they would now cost £49,000—and it was finally admitted that a school chapel would probably not be built.

In 1952 Miss Watt reached retiring age, having been at the school through one of the most testing and difficult periods of its history. The fact that it was now able to take in more girls than ever before, and had again extended its age range to cover the whole school age-span, speaks well of her administrative ability. She was also responsible for the formation of the Parent-Teacher Association which has been a flourishing institution ever since. Old girls of her period speak warmly of her concern for, and interest in, them, as well as of her fine teaching, and in saying farewell to Miss Watt the *Chronicle* gives a grateful and generous account of her particular contribution to the school.

Grace Watt—headmistress 1940-1952— However long the span of life granted to St Swithun's School may be—Et Floreat Aeterna—and however many headmistresses may be given to us, Miss Watt will have her own unique place among them all. None of her predecessors had to begin her tenure of office with no proper school buildings and the number of girls suddenly halved. No one else has had to endure six years of makeshift temporising among the scattered houses on St Giles' Hill; and then, on top of that, face all the delays, exasperations, and hopes deferred which were involved in getting the school buildings back again, and cleaning and preparing them for their proper use, and gradually (though astonishingly quickly) nursing the school to full health and strength. Her courage and faith carried her through and she carried the school. No doubt other headmistresses might have done the same, but none of them had to try. Circumstances

forced from her a particular and unique service to the school in those years, and in the
strength of what she did then her name will shine in the school's corporate memory.

The Council chose Miss Evans, an Oxford classicist and already a Headmistress, to
succeed her.

"HILARY WILL NEVER SWIM IF
SHE PERSISTS IN WALKING ALONG
THE BOTTOM..."

"HILARY IS IMPROVING SLOWLY..."

V

Miss Evans 1953-1973

When Miss Evans became Headmistress at the beginning of 1953, having returned from New Zealand, where she had been in charge of the Wellington Diocesan School, Britain was only just ending food rationing and other wartime controls. The Festival of Britain exhibition on the newly cleared South Bank site in London had been launched as a demonstration of a return to some kind of normality. For most girls' independent schools, the 1950s were however a period of rather tentative growth and development, which was not to quicken until the 1960s with their easy prosperity and rapid social change.

In Miss Evans's first term she was faced with one major change in the organisation of the school. The arrangements for the Junior School in Holy Trinity Vicarage in St Peter Street had never been very satisfactory. Shortly after the beginning of the spring term of 1953, the possibility of buying a much more suitable house in Sparkford Road was brought to the notice of the Council. They decided to make an offer for the property—Medecroft—which was accepted, and the house was to become the home of the Junior School for the next 12 years.

In the main, school staffing and facilities were still somewhat restricted in the aftermath of war: in particular, science teaching, the library and the sixth form all required attention. During the war the teaching of science had been limited by the lack of proper laboratories, and since the school had returned to its own buildings, both money and science teachers had been in short supply, putting a great strain on the resources of the department. Miss Evans felt that more attention must be paid to this area if the school was to regain its former reputation for all-round excellence. The library too had suffered from wartime restrictions on the publication of books, and an increased allowance would be necessary to cover the cost of restocking.

Both these matters were connected with, and to a certain extent contributory to, what Miss Evans felt to be the major problem—that of the sixth form. In a note to the Council in 1954 she expressed anxiety about the number of able girls leaving school either before entering the sixth form, or else after only one year in it. This was not a problem peculiar to St Swithun's; almost all girls' schools experienced it during the 1950s and 1960s and found themselves searching both for a cause and a cure. St Swithun's was, however, probably one of the earliest institutions to recognise the problem, which Miss Evans believed arose out of a generalised dissatisfaction with the way of life open to the sixth form girl.

It is felt, I am convinced, by some parents and girls, that such girls need a greater degree of intellectual stimulus, opportunity to work and be treated as students rather than as school girls, and less demands on their time by games and school responsibilities. It is a real difficulty to us that we have few girls in each house who are of University calibre—the situation of Hillcroft and Earlsdown also does not make it easy for their

58

Upper VI girls to spend as much time as one would wish either in the library or in general contact with other Upper VI girls in their free time.

She suggested that the school should think of providing a house or flat for sixth form girls with their own housemistress, where they could live in a more informal and relaxed manner, released from most school duties, with no compulsory games and wearing non-uniform clothes. A good deal of discussion in Council meetings followed over the next year, and though it proved relatively easy to relieve some of the strain on the science department and grant an increased allowance for the library, the matter of sixth form accommodation proved much more difficult to resolve. Tentative plans to utilise dining-room space in High House and Hyde, together with the caterer's flat at the top of the houses, or to build a new Headmistress's house and use the cottage, had to be laid aside with the introduction in 1955 of Equal Pay legislation which it was estimated would cost the school an additional £3,800, rising over the next five years. All that could be done immediately was to reduce the number of school duties expected of the Upper Sixth and to give them some special privileges, but the problem of isolation and the lack of really suitable working conditions remained.

Other problems, as well as financial ones, occupied a good deal of Council time. The difficulty of obtaining adequate domestic staff, especially cooks and caterers, was a constant preoccupation, and housemistresses and house matrons became increasingly difficult to replace as more and more women became professionally qualified. Another anxiety was a continuing imbalance between boarders and day girls; an increasing number of Winchester residents chose to send their daughters to the County High School, while boarding places were frequently oversubscribed.

If the 1950s were a difficult time for those administering the school, Old Girls of that period speak very happily of their time at school, unshadowed by such anxieties. Games were still an important feature of the school's life, especially during the era of Miss Angus and Miss de la Mare, who could strike terror into even the best games player's heart, and galvanise even the most unathletic into regular movement on the games field. When they left, Miss Margaret Roberts came as one of the two new P.E. staff. She is now the most senior full-time member of the staff, under whom the school has not only maintained but increased its reputation for games, especially lacrosse. The school was also very active in the field of music during this period, taking a distinguished part in the Winchester Music Festivals, and singing in the Winchester Music Club regularly, as well as putting on school concerts. Girls were also regular attenders at concerts given by famous performers either in the Guildhall or at the school itself.

1959 was the school's 75th anniversary, which was celebrated twice during the summer term. On 6 June, Old Girls and the present school joined together to enjoy an anniversary weekend with a great Thanksgiving Service in the Cathedral, followed by the launching of the 75th Anniversary Appeal by Sir John Woolfenden. The object of the appeal was to repay the mortgage raised to build the new school which yearly drained St Swithun's of much valuable income; it was also hoped that there would be enough money besides to make improvements to the present buildings. On 1 July the Duchess of Gloucester visited the school which showed itself off in fine style with displays of work and an outdoor physical education show of gym and dancing.

In many ways 1959 was to prove a turning point in the school's fortunes: the past 15 years since its 60th birthday had been ones of austerity and struggle, limited by the poverty of its resources. It was in this year that the Council received news of a welcome and most unexpected gift—a house (Upcot) in Quarry Road, which was bequeathed to St Swithun's by Mr. George Blore, together with a sum of money for its renovation. This legacy gave the school room to manoeuvre; to have its accommodation increased with little expenditure on its own part was exactly what it required at this stage, and Mr. Blore, an ex-College don who had taken a friendly interest in the school during his retirement, was a benefactor indeed. After very little discussion it was decided that Upcot should become a student house for nine girls; the sixth form were asked to name it and appropriately decided on Blore. It opened in September 1961 fully, indeed over-subscribed.

At the same time, in order to encourage more girls to stay on into the sixth form, two more courses were made available to them. A General Studies course was provided in the lower sixth particularly for those who were not staying on to take A levels, and in the upper sixth a Contemporary Studies course became compulsory, to avoid over-specialisation and a narrow concentration on the subjects to be offered at A level. All girls had to do some science and at least one modern language, as well as General Essay, English literature, divinity, and either history, art or music.

In the same year (1961) in which the benefit of Mr. Blore's request was first felt, the school received yet another legacy. It had been left another house and a large sum of money (estimated at about £40,000) in the will of Dr. Sybil Tremellen, subject to her husband's life interest. Dr. Tremellen lived on St Giles Hill, and, while having no direct connection with the school, had always taken an interest in it, and in particular with the recent Anniversary Appeal. It says much for the public image of St Swithun's at this time that two people with no very close links with the school should nevertheless think it worthy of such considerable benefactions. While the school could not benefit immediately, nevertheless the assurance of money to come gave the Council a greater sense of freedom in planning for the future.

A minor event in the same year was a change in some items of school uniform, including the abandonment of the tie but the retention of the summer hat. This latter provoked a letter in the *Chronicle*:

Dear Editor,
Why do we have to be so old-fashioned at this school? Why can't we be more up-to-date with our school uniform? Take, for example, the school hats. Maybe they were fashionable when they were first designed but we must realise that times have changed, and if Christian Dior could see us, he would die of shock! How nice it would be to have cheerful and attractive hats! The 'Gigi' style hats and boaters are very smart and suit everyone. If we are caught in a storm of rain, which is all too likely with English weather, our hats form into the most peculiar shapes. I'm sure we would not mind wearing summer hats half as much if they were not so old-fashioned and depressing. Outsiders jeer at the sight of our hats. Why should we be the laughing-stock of Winchester?—
Yours sincerely,
CHAPEAU, M. Vb

and this response from the Editor:

If Chapeau can produce a hat which will suit equally, elegant Sixth formers, over-weight Vs, tiny IVs, buns, fuzzy fringes and lank straight locks, and which will remain fashionable for at least ten years, so as to spare parents' pockets, the School authorities will give her a complete new school uniform free as a reward – Ed.

Another matter connected with dress which caused much aggravation at this time was hair, a subject which is exploited in a parody of a song instantly recognisable to all Old St Swithuns' girls:

Hair

Thirteen years on, with hair dyed and longer,
Beehive and Bouffant, no glimpses of slides,
When you look back and regretfully wonder
What it was like to be short back and sides;
Then it may be, there will often come o'er you
Glimpses of fringes, but half an inch long,
Visions of girlhood shall float then before you,
Echoes of scissors snipping round and along.

Twenty years on, when married and older,
Sparser in hair, and with girls of your own,
Longing to wear hair down to the shoulder,
What will it help you that once you were young?
Will you have the strength to cut it and tell them—
'Everyone knows that rules have to be kept?'
Won't you remember that when you were younger,
Forced to the hairdressers, you bitterly wept?

These two contributions to the *Chronicle* are minor manifestations of deep sociological changes which were taking place in the 1960s, and which affected boarding schools as much as other institutions. With so-called 'full employment' the earning capacity of school leavers increased enormously and a whole teenage culture sprang up to exploit their sudden affluence. They were made to feel, by extensive advertising campaigns, that they were a most sought-after and valuable section of society. At the same time the adult population also experienced an increase in spending power and the consequent sense of independence, which communicated itself quickly to their children.

Assumptions about standards and morality which had been taken for granted began to be questioned in this general atmosphere of material well-being and freedom, and it was no longer possible for schools to assume that the majority of their pupils would obey the rules without question. Boarding school pupils, particularly, found the adjustment from home life to school increasingly difficult: at home during the holidays they were leading an almost adult existence, with limited parental control, and found difficult the transformation into the traditional schoolgirl during term time. This was particularly so when, as at St Swithun's, the day girls were a constant reminder of the possibilities of home life. Gradually, changes were made to meet the changing situation; in 1964 some housemistresses made arrangements for their senior girls to have more freedom in meeting and entertaining boys known to them. The sixth form abandoned uniform in 1965, and games became voluntary. Miss Evans asked Dr. Zaida Hall whether she would come to talk to the senior girls and a series of lectures entitled 'Design for Living' were organised to help them cope with the greater freedom in personal relations which now obtained. These lectures have been continued, and have now become a very valuable part of the school's extra-curricular programme. The school found, too, that the day girls themselves were a source of some anxiety; not all parents or staff found it easy to cope with the increased freedom their daughters were demanding, and felt that they were not always choosing their friends or their leisure activities very wisely. In the town, too, these girls were not always representing the school in an appropriate style. However, Miss Evans and the Council quite properly felt that while the school would give every help possible in instilling the need for good manners and sensible behaviour, it was not desirable that it should attempt to control the out-of-school activities of day girls.

The process of adjustment was necessarily a gradual one; girls' boarding schools are not institutions which can adapt to a social revolution very easily, since the majority of them were designed to meet the needs of a social structure which was very different from that coming into being in the 1960s and 1970s, and which was not universally welcomed either by parents or staff. One way in which the school could help to give an increased sense of freedom to its pupils was by extending the range of extra-curricular activities available to them. The Mission Committee became the Social Service Council, and while retaining its traditional support for the U.G.S., a good deal of the school activity was concentrated on local needs such as visiting the hospitals and the St John Almshouses, and giving practical help to old people. During 1969 and 1970 some girls joined with other Winchester schools in an archaeological excavation organised by the College in the grounds of Lankhills School. The College began to lend its badminton courts to the school on a regular basis, and, perhaps, also as a sign of the times, cricket was abandoned as a compulsory game in 1963. Judo was first introduced in 1968, and had an immediate success; in 1969 a pair from St Swithun's represented Hampshire in the British Schools' Judo Association Championships at the Crystal Palace and were placed second in the Intermediate Section, and in the following two years, two different pairs became the National Schoolgirl Champions in turn. In 1971 one of the participants wrote an account for the *Chronicle* in which she said 'That evening we performed in front of the Mayor and Mayoress of Warley, the Japanese Ambassador and several other V.I.P.s. As we were making our last bow, the Japanese Ambassador stood up and bowed to us; we have been told that this was a great honour, as it is rare for a Japanese man to bow to a woman, let alone stand up to and bow to her'.

Miss Armit retired in December 1964 having been head of the Classics Department since 1928. Although she was regarded with a good deal of awe by many generations of St Swithun's girls, as Miss Evans said in her obituary notice when she died in 1976, 'no member of staff maintained a larger correspondence with Old Girls, and this is a testimony not only to the admiration but also to the affection in which she was held'. Miss Evans wrote of her marvellous record in public examinations: 'no one failed, and she took endless trouble and gave unstintingly of her time to those needing extra help. But Miss Armit's influence at St Swithun's did not end with her classroom teaching: far from it. She was always form-mistress of the 13-14 age group, that most difficult of all stages. Her first remark to each new generation in September was "There are two things I will not tolerate, bad manners and draughts". The windows in her classroom were always shut: and she supervised dinner in the Junior dining-room, where her insistence on good table manners and proper conversational efforts from those who sat next to her were not appreciated, perhaps, so much at that time as in later life'. A present governor of the school says that Miss Armit's training has helped her through many a sticky dinner party. A legend which there is no reason to doubt, records that one of her favourite sayings was 'Whatever goes into your mouth must never come out'. The careless would swallow their prune stones rather than risk her rebuke.

In the 1960s, too, two other activities which were to become a regular feature of the school's life, appeared on the school calendar. In 1966 the first small party went on an educational cruise in the Mediterranean during the Easter holidays, and a year or two later the school began to make use of the facilities of 'Celmi' an Adventure Centre rented by Stanbridge Earls School in the Dysinni Valley in Wales, and to which parties of girls, together with pupils from other schools, have gone regularly during term-time ever since. This composite account of the experience of Celmi is taken from a later edition of *Chronicle*:

Celmi

The Visitors Book at Celmi includes the names of many from St Swithun's. This year's visit by 34 Middle Fifths and two staff was greatly enjoyed, despite capricious weather. Celmi, though more often than not uncomfortable, wet, chilly, strenuous and exhausting, offers a positive and challenging experience. The landscape is varied and beautiful—and provides a superb laboratory for geographical field-work, in which we had expert and well documented guidance. Activities ranged from a farm visit, a town trail of Dolgellau with its cattle market, to map-reading over a course designed to tax intelligence, observation, tenacity, team work and stamina. Other exercises tested personal qualities of precision (rock climbing), balance (canoeing), trust (abseiling) and fortitude (camping out on a windy October night). All were carefully monitored and supervised, with a ratio of one staff member to every three participants.

Accounts follow of two of the most testing activities.

The Slate Mines At Night

When we arrived at the slate mines, we were taught how to use all the equipment and given our safety helmets. We had to trudge up a hill, but we couldn't see a thing. While a few of the instructors set everything up, Berry taught us about the slate and the history of the mines in Aberdovey. We entered a long tunnel, after having put on all sorts of harnesses and clips. There were few torches, so I couldn't see where I was going. At the end of the tunnel we entered a large cavern where slate had once been mined. We walked on to an even larger cavern and then down a short, dark tunnel where we were told to sit and wait while all the equipment for a sixty foot drop in the dark was fixed up. I had to wait about an hour before it was my turn. I peeped over the edge and gasped: it seemed such a long way down. It took a while before I was finally coaxed over the edge. To start with it was very 'scary'. However, once you were half way down, you were to jump and an instructor pulled you on to a ledge. Then you had to make your way down a small hole to another instructor waiting at the bottom. The mines were very wet and, when we left, we had to wade out through the tunnel, finally arriving at the bottom of the hill.

Rock Climbing

After being securely strapped into our climbing gear, we clambered apprehensively down a path towards the shingle beach. When the party reached the chosen cliff, we were carefully given climbing instructions and a brief demonstration by Will who whizzed up the cliff, quite at ease. Excitedly queues were formed. We were shown how to climb the rock. Then I was fixed to a safety rope, so rather tentatively I began to climb. It was not as easy as I had imagined. The rope kept getting in the way and there were not enough footholds. The sides sloped inwards and the holes were so small I could hardly fit my big toe in! However, once I had mastered the basic skills, I really enjoyed it. By the time I got to the hardest climb I was fairly confident. Then disaster struck. I got stuck half way up. My foot was sideways on in a crack and this was the only grip I had. I stayed like this for about three minutes before I managed to get to the top, but even this could not dampen my enthusiasm. I really enjoyed it and would urge anyone to have a go!

One other development of the 1960s is worth mentioning; although it does not relate strictly to the history of the school it is of interest as an extension of opportunities available to Old Girls of the school, and it did produce one or two contributions to *Chronicle* which merit inclusion the school history. This was V.S.O.—Voluntary Service Overseas—which in its early years selected school-leavers as well as recent graduates to go and work for a year—often as teachers—in the undeveloped countries. In 1965 Jane Maulden wrote from Nigeria where she was teaching:

If you can picture power and poverty, an annual income of several thousand pounds and one of thirty pounds, cats-eyes and street lights illuminating the stagnant gutter along each street, upturning winklepickers and Oxfam advertisements, a chief's private Methodist chapel but alongside it his juju shrine, 'highlife' band music and the pulse of drums at night, dense tropical forest and arid desert country, hot sun, thunderstorms and clear, still nights, and last—tribalism stronger even than nationalism—you will perhaps have an idea of the memories I will bring home with me from a small bush town in Nigeria. The clatter of washbuckets for washing at dawn, the sound of rush hand-brooms on the compound paths, the rush to the dining hall with plate, mug, spoon and water-bottle and the smell of native soup, the ancient harmonium, the one netball that leaks, backward running races, French songs and pidgin English, kerosene lamps for working in the evening, the arrival of a science graduate who draws a test tube on the blackboard but has none to use, despair when a lesson ends and nothing seems to have been achieved and hope when someone at last grasps an algebra problem—all these must be typical of many Nigerian Mission grammar shcools which are modelled on the English system, but with a five- or six-year course leading to the School Certificate, the equivalent of 'O' level. With bride prices still prevalent, a grammar school education, although a great sacrifice for almost all families, is an investment, for an educated first wife is much in demand. As a result, such importance is placed on the certificate examination that the sixth form, whose ages range from 19-22 or 23, become quite desperate, as the time draws near, to acquire knowledge that will help them pass.

Sarah Gladwell sent this account from Enugu in East Nigeria, where she was teaching as a graduate in the leading girls' government school:

Many things struck me as strange at first: teachers are known as 'tutors' and the pupils are called 'students'. The 'students' get up at 5 a.m. and all the classrooms and dormitories are scrubbed and brushed before lessons begin at 8 a.m. At first, I was fascinated by the girls' hair styles: they wear their hair plaited into a number of spiky plaits all over their heads, and black cotton is wound firmly round each plait so that it sticks straight up in the air! I am teaching French, which is at present a very 'fashionable' subject in Nigeria. The need for French is great, as around us on all sides are French-speaking West African countries. Teaching difficulties are considerable, as I find 'students' tend to translate in their heads from Ibo (their own language) to English and finally to French! So it is not surprising when they get muddled half way and come out with 'mba' (Ibo for 'no') instead of 'non'. As Enugu is very much in the centre of things, numerous other jobs crop up besides normal school teaching: once a week I have an extra-mural German class in the town for students who hope to study German and want to equip themselves with some knowledge of the language beforehand. Nigerian Broadcasting runs French radio programmes and I have to help with these and also with occasional television French lessons. My greatest surprise came, however, when I was asked to give French lessons to the Premier of E. Nigeria, Dr. M. Okpwa, and all his ministers. I could hardly believe it, when I arrived at the Premier's Lodge on my Honda and was taken to the 'classroom'—a magnificent, air-conditioned hall, where at least 25 chiefs dressed in their colourful Nigerian robes and hats were assembled. They showed great enthusiasm and were thrilled when they could say 'Bonjour' and ask each other questions about the objects in the room.

With the opening of Blore House in 1961, a beginning was made to improve the living and working conditions of the sixth form, which had caused Miss Evans a good deal of thought and concern since she became Headmistress in 1953. It also brought into the school a little extra revenue, and enabled it to use some of the money raised by the 75th Anniversary Appeal to begin a programme of building which has, in fact, been continuing ever since. By the beginning of the 1960s the school was very short of teaching space as its numbers had been increasing all the time. The Art department's premises were not really suitable for the modern style of Art and Craft teaching, but the rooms would be perfectly suitable for classrooms, so in 1962 the Council commissioned the building of a new cedar-clad Studio and Crafts room, its first piece of building since the war. The new building cost just over £8,000 and was of suitably modest proportions.

Plans were then produced for a two-stage project, developing as funds permitted, for new cloakrooms and for dining facilities. In the post-war world, with little and expensive domestic help, feeding the school was a constant anxiety: each boarding house on St Giles Hill still went 'home' for its meals, and day girls and the two 'new' boarding houses only were fed in the main school buildings. The first stage of the plan was for a new cloakroom with a new kitchen above it, with, at a later stage, provision for a new dining room and further cloakrooms. This would immediately release sufficient space to be able to introduce central feeding for the whole school at least at lunch time. This was financed by an extension of the school's loan facilities, as it was felt that it would now be possible to finance the interest on the loan out of current income. The building was ready shortly after the beginning of the spring term of 1966 and for the first time in its history the school ate its midday meal together, rather than separating into houses.

In 1966 yet another new building was completed. During the early years of the 1960s there was a slow but steady decline in numbers at Medecroft, which had never done more than barely pay its way. Although it provided for an obvious need in the town, its awkward position made it expensive to run. Its separation from the main school facilities began to tell against it, and in 1964 the decision was reluctantly taken to close it in March 1966, and to transfer the Preparatory Department to St Giles Hill as an annexe to the Junior Boarding House, LeRoy. But then Miss Evans and the then Bursar, Miss Gaukroger, had an inspiration. Why not use the money the school hoped to raise by the sale of Medecroft to build a new Junior School in the main school grounds, using pre-fabricated units to save costs? It was estimated that this would cost something in the region of £12,000: an advantageous sale of Medecroft to King Alfred's Training College meant that in the end the buildings could be rather more extensive than originally planned, with a Games Room and Music Room in addition to the basic classrooms. The Old Girls Association very generously gave a gymnasium which could be used by seniors also in out-of-school hours, for such things as fencing, dancing and judo. With better buildings, and a share in the main school's playing fields and swimming pool, numbers in the Junior school began to rise quite rapidly, and its future was no longer in doubt when the new buildings were opened in the autumn of 1966.

It was, perhaps, sad that this revival of the Junior school's fortunes should have coincided with Miss Hobson's retirement, as she had been so closely connected with the new girls in the Senior school, many of whom she had known as Juniors. An attempt to summarise her contribution to the school between 1929 and 1966 produced the following incredible list which appeared in the *Chronicle*, 1965/66. 'Miss Hobson, 1929/1966. M. and Senior School. Taught French, Needlework, Divinity, English. Form Mistress Lower IV; introduced all new girls gently into the ways of the school and protected them from the wrath of Praefects, and from detentions and confiscations. School Sacristan; looked after the Quiet Room and School Evensong, produced flowers, washed and ironed the Chaplain's vestments, instructed the Servers, taught most children their Catechism. Advisor (an inadequate title) to the Social Service Committee; was responsible for the organisation of all the work done by the school for the U.G.S., U.S.P.G., the Appeals Committee, the Harvest Festivals, the making of blankets, the raising of money, the entertainment of children from the Mission Settlement, or old people from St John's Almshouses. With all this, Miss Hobson was officially a part-time member of staff; but never was so much done for so many by one person.' Luckily her 'retirement' was only relative, and until very recently she has continued to give help with dyslexic teaching and invigilating and was an invaluable source of information for the history of the school in the last fifty years.

The Tremellen bequest, about which the Council had known since 1961, bcame available in 1966 after Mr. Tremellen's death in February. The school had now at its disposal, for the first time in its history, a considerable capital sum not already committed, and it took the Council some time to work out the most advantageous way of using it. It was soon agreed that in principle the ultimate object should be to dispose of the St Giles' Hill boarding houses, growing more and more uneconomic with increasing maintenance costs and lack of domestic help, and provide new boarding accommodation on the main school site.

Any rapid decision about detail was made more difficult since the Public Schools Commission, set up in 1965 to consider 'the best way of integrating the Public Schools with the State system of education', was conducting its enquiries, and until the publication in 1969 of the first part of its Report there was considerable doubt as to whether the independent schools had any future at all! In 1969 the Council made enquiries as to the cost of two large new boarding houses and the figure produced, £485,000, showed that this project was far beyond their means. This gave Miss Evans the opportunity to press the claims of a new sixth form centre, possibly with boarding accommodation, thus providing some spare boarding places in the existing houses. Although some members of the Council and Staff felt misgivings about removing the senior girls from their houses, it was finally agreed that this was the way in which the Tremellen money could best be used, and that an Appeal should also be launched to enable the building of the sixth form house, to be coupled with necessary improvements in the St Giles' Hill houses.

So the idea of Finlay was born. At first it was envisaged as a free standing house, but the total money available was not sufficient for this and it was largely due to Miss Evans' ingenuity and determination that it was fitted in on its present site completing the quadrangle on the north-west of the main building, providing 24 study-bedrooms and common room, with study space for the whole sixth form.

The bulk of the present school's contribution to the appeal on this occasion was raised by a sponsored 15-mile walk, in which Miss Evans herself took part, extracting considerable sums of money from a captive audience on Parents' Day. She subsequently described the walk for the *Chronicle*:

The organisation beforehand was done, in the field by Miss Pope to whom the success of the walk is very largely due, in the offices by Miss Gaukroger, Miss Winter and their Staffs. Miss Pope and Miss Thomas twice walked the projected route to make sure that there would be no walking on main roads, that no tracks were impassable, and that there were suitable places for stewards. Then Sunday, 27th September, started with a Service in the Hall, at which the hymn of the Hampshire Countryside was appropriately sung. By ten o'clock, the front of school was gay with coloured anoraks and sweaters. Six buses were lined up, surrounded by 500 walkers, accompanied by what seemed like an equivalent number of dogs. We all set off into thick mist and were dropped at the staging points, two miles, five miles, twelve miles and fifteen miles away from school. I cannot describe the whole walk by mile, though I shall long remember all its details: the Hampshire countryside on a morning of late summer, privet, hips, haws, spindle, old man's beard, the occasional hazel and beech just beginning to turn; no spectacular views, because it was still misty on Old Winchester Hill; but it gradually cleared, and the day became warm, so that the occasional handful of blackberries was welcome; coming round a turn of the road, there, where three lanes met, was the school van, with Mr. and Mrs. Green giving out lunch bags and fizzy drinks, and even providing tea for the Staff, and a chair (!) for me. Every time we emerged from a track on to a driveable road, there we found a member of staff supplying drink, and encouragement. Then on to Kilmeston and Beauworth, down a long hill under a tall avenue of beeches, over Gander Down and Cheesfoot Head, back through Chilcomb village and up the steep hillside to the Cottage. There I obediently went in and telephoned my safe arrival before actually marching down the school drive. And what a triumphal march it proved to be: flags over the front door (by courtesy of the Bursar), a band playing Colonel Bogey (by courtesy of a gramophone), some Wykehamist friends shouting 'Encore' (did they really think I could ever do it again!) and the drive lined with members of Council, parents, staff, girls and (of course) dogs.

Finally the money. The venture raised £3,405, of which £1,218 was contributed by my personal sponsors, to whom I am deeply grateful, not least for their kind messages of congratulation, and for many additions to the sums originally promised.

The article is accompanied by a splendid photograph of Miss Evans, looking in the last few strides as if she was just starting out, rather than finishing the full 15 miles.

Once started, the new VI form house was completed in just about a year, and was opened formally on 5 February 1972 by Miss Finlay just two days before her 90th birthday. Without notes, and standing (to aid clarity of thought, she said) she spoke in a marvellously clear and youthful voice 'My Lord, Mr. Dean, Members of Council, Ladies and Gentlemen. I am very happy to be here today to open this VIth Form House for I feel that it would have the approval of the founders of St Swithun's school. It was their intention that "true religion and sound learning" was to be the aim of this foundation in 1884, and I believe that aim has remained unchanged. There is no need to enlarge on this since the School records over the years give proof that many from here have gone out into the world to serve God and their fellows, and I would add to create an honourable reputation for sound learning at the older Universities. In an age when modern gadgets and dislike of effort are in insidious ways reducing the need for human mental activity fears are openly being expressed that serious thinking and reading are being undermined. Surely then this is a time to encourage learning and this new House with its facilities for quiet study and discussion should do so, while the increased opportunity for social intercourse will be a further step towards the freer life which lies ahead. I fell in love with the school, just two years younger than myself, fifty-six years ago. Now Finlay House will always have a specially warm place in my heart. There are many stories about opening speeches, which should be marked by brevity, though we cannot all emulate the lady, a classical scholar, who suddenly bereft of words said simply EPHPHATHA. Our own Princess Royal opening the main building was nearly as brief for at that time she rarely spoke at length merely stating her pleasure in announcing the place open, but she made up for any disappointment there may have been by asking for a day's holiday for the whole school. Not being Royalty I cannot do that but please accept my best wishes for this delightful Finlay House which I now declare open without further words.'

One of the first occupants of Finlay recorded these impressions ... 'Whatever are we going to say about Finlay? Well ... Well, what are we going to say? Sherry, Sunshine Corner, smell of toast and coffee, powercuts and concerts around the candles, the silent night-black prowler, showers at 2.00 a.m., Private Eye and portable television, muttered midnight conversations, thin walls, through which Blake is heard intermingled with Bolan, punctual lateness for meals. Also of course, there was work; and A-levels ... matters which, contrary to popular belief, were not entirely forgotten.'

Once Finlay was completed it was possible to dispense with one, at least, of the older boarding houses on St Giles Hill and to make some considerable improvements to the others. In the end it was decided that Hillcroft should be the one to be sold, and that Hillcroft residents should move into LeRoy taking their name with them, and that Chilcomb should become the Junior boarding house taking the name LeRoy. It had been thought that Blore could also be sold, but during the later years of the 1960s Miss Evans had had a steady stream of requests to take weekly boarders, and it was decided to use Blore as a weekly boarding house from September 1972. Once started the scheme prospered so vigorously that weekly boarders soon overflowed into all the boarding houses.

As the time drew near for Miss Evans to retire, two very personal honours came her way; in May 1970 she became President of the Association of Girls' Boarding Schools, and in June the same year she was admitted as a lay reader in Winchester Cathedral, one of the very few women to be so honoured. One cannot end an account of her headmistress-ship either without recalling the splendid series of school plays put on during the 20 years at St Swithun's in many of which she was involved as producer; 'Noah' by André Obey, 'Holy Night', 'Lets make an Opera', 'A Midsummer Night's Dream', 'The Immortal Lady', 'The Happy Prince' an opera by Malcolm Williamson and 'Tobias and the Angel'.

Even in the last year of her appointment, Miss Evans was still pressing on with building schemes, in this case a new Dining Hall which would complete the building in the Quadrangle which contained the kitchen, cloakrooms and Finlay, all of which had been undertaken during her time at St Swithun's. Despite a good deal of misgiving initially, both on her part and that of many members of the Council, it was decided to introduce cafeteria feeding, which would be a saving of staff, time and space: the fear of deteriorating manners and standards proved to be quite unfounded, and the space thus released allowed a total reorganisation of the library in the Old Dining Rooms, together with the provision of one new classroom and a much improved staff room in the Old Library. Thus Miss Evans retired with apparent undiminished energy.

At the Old Girls' Association Dinner in June 1973, one of her Old Girls, Sylvia Lush, now Lady Limerick, spoke most gracefully of all her contributions to the school, her care for and development of the sixth form in Blore and Finlay, and in the inauguration of special sixth form courses, the quality of religious life which she encouraged, the material development of the school in its new buildings and especially in the new Junior school and the studio and 'her cheerfulness and zest for life, her sense of humour, integrity and her power to continue it to the end until it be thoroughly finished'. On a more flippant note I should like to compare St Swithun's loss with that of Mr. Barnum's of the circus company who, on being told of the untimely departure of the clown who was fired from the barrel of the cannon, commented 'How sad! Its going to be so difficult to find another person of his calibre'.

Difficult or not, the Council succeeded in appointing Miss Olwen Davies, a mathematician and then Headmistress of St Mary's Hall, Brighton, under whose care the school has made an impressive advance in all spheres so that it comes into its centenary year full of prestige and vigour.

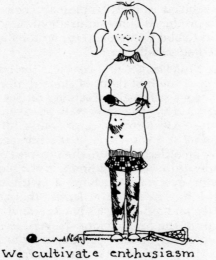

We cultivate enthusiasm
for a wide range of
physical activities: lacrosse

VI

Miss Davies, 1973-

Miss Davies' appointment became effective in September 1973 and coincided almost exactly with the oil crisis following the Arab-Israeli war of that year, which has had such a profound effect on our economy, amongst other things trebling school fees in ten years. The immediate effect was an increase of nearly 20 per cent in expenditure in the school year 1973-4, a matter which caused some concern since the new Dining Hall was not completed and equipped until the spring of 1974 when increased costs were already making themselves felt. It was much appreciated, and if the cooking and staffing arrangements caused some headaches to begin with, this was evidently not noticed by the author of this article in the *Chronicle*: 'St Swithun's now owns a canteen, and, looking back on our previous eating arrangements, it is difficult to imagine how the kitchen staff coped. The canteen has changed our eating habits; we should be bursting with vitamin C, since we consume three times as many vegetables. In spite of this, this system is more economical and the general opinion is that the food has improved greatly. One amusing aspect of the canteen is the menu posted outside. Pork chops are now billed as 'Pork Tropicana'. The wide choice (salads and 2 main hot courses) has also produced some amusement. One girl in the sixth form, when Toad-in-the-Hole and Rabbit Casserole were on the menu, was asked "Rabbit or Toad, love?" I think she had salad!'

The other major event of Miss Davies' first year was the transferring of the library from its old room at the top of the first flight of stairs to the newly-released Dining Room on the same floor. 'Never again shall we saunter carelessly into a library, seize a book from one of its shelves and nonchalantly walk out again: for the labours of the school, and especially of the Sixth form—and, of course, of the indefatigable Miss Pemberton—have made us all too conscious of the immense toil involved in the creation and maintenance of an orderly library. The prospect of transferring the entire contents of the three libraries into their new home in the old dining-rooms seemed daunting at first, but with everyone pitching in with much enthusiasm and willingness to help—for the first half-hour at least!—the task was completed in a creditably short time. Our leg and arm muscles have certainly suffered from carrying armloads of books down from the top corridor. Nevertheless, our waistlines have undoubtedly benefited from our frequently bending over to retrieve books that had fallen from toppling piles. These and other mistakes were made, naturally enough, but with the result that the work was not monotonous; for scarcely five minutes passed without a smile or giggle, of horror or amusement, emanating from a corner, where some unfortunate wretch had found out that she had put an entire shelf in back to front—or had made out cards for fiction on non-fiction-coloured cardboard. And adding enormously to the amusement was the discovery of such literary works as "The Life History of an English Spinster" and "The Romance of Arithmetic", together with many other equally fascinating tomes of which we had hitherto been ignorant.'

Miss Davies' second year opened in a much more dramatic fashion. On the night of 2 October 1974 the Junior school burnt down: the fire was first seen at about 10.30 p.m. when a passer-by noticed it and told the caretaker. Almost at the same moment Miss Davies saw it and, in running over to school, fell over the low chains at the front gate, breaking her wrist and bruising herself badly. The fire engines arrived very quickly but only managed to save three classrooms and a small cloakroom. The hall, staff room, main cloakroom and rooms 1 and 2 were completely burnt out, and all staff records and library books were lost. Despite her injuries, Miss Davies, together with the Head of the Junior school and another member of staff, started at 7 a.m. to telephone all parents of Junior school girls, to ask that the children be kept at home for the moment: the Senior school and staff were confronted by the blackened ruins as they arrived for the day's work. In an astonishingly short space of time the Junior school was operating again, thanks to a great deal of hard work by the staff. The three top forms were back at work by the following Monday and the rest of the Juniors by the middle of the week: a portable lavatory and one portable classroom arrived within a few days and two more Portakabins followed. Almost immediately donations began to come in, many of them specifically for re-establishing the library, and the amount of good-will generated was very heartening.

While the rebuilding of the Junior school was under discussion it was suggested that the new building should include boarding accommodation for the Junior boarders, thus enabling LeRoy to be sold and the school's occupancy of St Giles Hill further reduced. This proposal was adopted, and the new Junior school, a neat brick building, went up fast in the summer of 1975 and was ready for use during the autumn term. As usual the present school made its contribution: a sponsored swim was organised to pay for a specially-sprung Gym; it produced £2,500, to which and additional £750 was given by the P.T.A. The current Upper IV girls carved a relief on the outside of the new building and the Old Girls' Association also raised over £800, a very generous sum of money. The boarding accommodation occupied the whole of the first floor and contained such up-to-date conveniences as bunk beds and duvets.

By 1976 increasing numbers had brought the Senior school up to 400, the maximum which the existing classrooms and cloakrooms could house. It was time to take stock and make plans for the next few years. From discussions and lists of priorities, various points emerged: there was still a tendency, particularly among local girls, to leave at the end of the Upper V year to take 'A' level courses elsewhere, usually at a sixth-form college. While the reason for this was often financial it was felt that it was very important for the school to retain as many of its pupils into the VI form as possible in order to continue to attract first class staff, and that the widening of the syllabus to include more subjects available at 'A' level was something which should be considered.

Musically the school suffered from having its facilities scattered round the whole building, and better equipment was needed; if a separate music centre could be built this would not only focus more attention on the school's music but would also free valuable space in the main building for classrooms and cloakrooms, a little more room for staff, and more rooms for Finlay. It was accepted as a matter of principle that the school should continue to try to concentrate the boarding houses on the main site and gradually get rid of the St Giles Hill houses. The school was likely to lose some of the playing fields to the M3 extension and space had to be allocated to making good the losses. In the short term, two comparatively minor improvements were undertaken; a covered way at first floor level to link the dining room and Finlay with the main school, and the removal of the San to the main building by altering and extending the domestic staff flats at the back of Hyde Abbey and High House. To finance this, the old San, the school's first building on its present site, was sold in 1978.

It was at this stage that the school's policy of continuous development and extension over the previous ten years began to take effect, engendering it with a spirit of self-confidence that was evident both to those in the school and to prospective parents. Miss Davies reported to the Council that many more girls were staying on into the sixth form—numbers increased to more than ninety, having previously been fifty to sixty—and that Finlay was likely to overflow in September 1978. In 1978 the school gained 16 University places, of which one was a Cambridge Scholarship and two were Exhibitions, one each at Oxford and Cambridge. In 1979 the number of girls taking 'A' levels rose from an average of about 25 to 44 and has remained at that level ever since; indeed in 1982 there were 24 University places and 49 successful 'A' level candidates. Both 'O' and 'A' level results have been consistently far above the national average. In 1981 the pass rate at 'O' level was over 87 per cent with 73 per cent gaining 'A' or 'B' grades, and at 'A' level the overall pass rate was nearly 90 per cent with 58 per cent gaining 'A' or 'B' grades. There has been a steady increase, too, in the number of candidates offering science or mathematics; currently 50 per cent of 'A' level candidates are including science in their choice of subjects.

In games, too, the school struck a good patch. In 1977 four Lacrosse teams went to the All England Schools Lacrosse Tournament at Merton Abbey, and all four figured in the final placings in their classes; the 1st XII and the Junior XII both won their sections, and the 2nd XII were runners-up in their competition, while the under 14s came third. In 1981 the Junior XII won again and in 1982 the 1st XII won their competition. In all these years team players were selected for Hampshire Junior team and the West of England team, and in 1982 three players were selected for training with the Junior England Squad, one of whom became Junior England goal-keeper while still in the Upper V.

Other sports had their successes too. In 1978 in Judo, the school provided one of the Southern Team for the National Womens' Team Championships, and in 1982 a member of the Great Britain under 20 squad in Fencing, as well as several territorial team members. The under 16-Fencing team won the Portslade under-16 International Trophy. Golf and Archery were both introduced in 1980 and in 1983 a member of the school won the under-18 Girls Simple Bow section at the British Schools Archery Competition.

It is indeed difficult to find an area in which the school has not shown an extraordinary vigour in the last five years. The number and scope of school expeditions has grown steadily; the 'A' level historians have been both to France (several times) and the Low Countries with some Geographers, and in the spring of 1982 a party from the Upper school went to the United States, staying part of the time with private families in Allentown. Each year Mrs. Duff has taken an enthusiastic party on a Mediterranean educational cruise. School plays grow more and more ambitious and professional involving large numbers of people; 'Oliver' in 1977 seemed to involve almost the whole school, and it has been followed by 'Oh What a Lovely War', 'A Midsummer Night's Dream', 'Charlie and the Chocolate Factory' and most ambitiously in 1982, the opera 'Dido and Aeneas', when the Staff and some boys from the College also took part. Art and photography are flourishing, and social services, after a rather blank period, have shown much more vigour with, as their main concerns, old people in Winchester and a school for handicapped children in Brighton. A brave attempt to establish the Duke of Edinburgh's Award Scheme has been hampered by lack of outside support.

The visible sign of all this energy and well-being is the fine series of new buildings which have gone up since 1978. At the end of 1977 the Council decided to build the music school. The site chosen was between the rebuilt Junior school and the art studio, and the exterior was designed to harmonise with the reddish brick of the Junior school. Inside, the building contains a recital room, which has proved large enough to accommodate performances of a form play, class rooms, nine teaching and practice rooms and four small practice rooms; even so it is a hard-worked building, providing for the needs of about 300 instrumentalists, and it was given a fine official opening by Meredith Davies and the school musicians.

By the time the music school was completed the Council felt in a strong enough financial position to consider further building projects. Two evident needs presented themselves for consideration; the removal of the remaining boarding houses from St Giles Hill and better sports facilities. As well as the rather old-fashioned accommodation in the Hill houses, they suffered from the disadvantage of being vulnerable to the increasing hooliganism of the times, a condition which was somewhat eased by the employment of regular Securicor patrols. In 1979 the Council decided that all the Hill houses should be replaced eventually by two boarding houses, each designed to take 45 girls, and that the first one should be put into commission immediately. Prohibitive costs made it impossible to consider repeating the design of High House and Hyde Abbey, and in any case the site originally intended for them in the 1930s had been put to other uses. Instead, a somewhat revolutionary design of pre-fabricated units was chosen, based on a Swedish method of construction, and intended to conserve energy. The building is timber-framed, with a layer of rock wool insulation in the exterior walls and roof, and it is faced with a warm-coloured brick. It is long and low and faces west across the games field, backed by a line of firs down the side drive. It provides sleeping space for 46 girls, 30 in cubicles and 16 in single rooms; there are also three common rooms, a library, a games room and a kitchen for the use of the girls. Also incorporated in it is a small chapel for general use by the whole school. It is a building which has aroused much professional interest and seems to be thoroughly popular with its present inhabitants. It has taken the name of Earlsdown and also includes the old members of Blore, enabling these two older houses to be sold to help pay for the rebuilding.

While the new Earlsdown was being built, the sports facilities came under further pressure; three tennis courts were lost because of the extension of the by-pass to bring it up to motorway standard, and though they were re-built at government expense, they took up ground which had been used for other purposes. The growing size of the Junior school meant that their gym was less available to the Senior school, and the range of sporting activities was being further extended, so rather than embark on the second new boarding house immediately, funds were diverted to the building of a new Sports Hall which was completed in 1982 and sited to the north of High House and Hyde Abbey.

Now, with the rapid increase in the sciences over the last two or three years, the whole structure of science teaching in the school, and its resources, is under review, as it has become clear that the present laboratories are no longer adequate.

So St Swithun's enters its Centenary Year in a very healthy state, with its numbers over 500 since 1982. One more development must be commented upon. After a lapse of a considerable number of years, the school is once again taking boys, not only in the sixth-form cookery classes where there are a number of enthusiastic cooks from the College, but in the Junior school, where a nursery class has been established, including a number of small boys.

"SUSANNAH'S COORDINATION LEAVES SOMETHING TO BE DESIRED..."

"HENRIETTA WOULD IMPROVE IF SHE PAID MORE ATTENTION TO THE GAME..."

VII

The School Today

Inevitably the more recent history of the school lacks the charm and historical curiosity of the early years and tends to lapse into a rather bald catalogue of events. But for the historians of the future, as well as for past generations, it is possible to give some account of what it felt like to be in the school at the end of its first hundred years; so here are comments, first of all from the youngest members of the school, then from a member of the Upper VI, and finally from senior members of staff.

First Impressions
'To tell you the truth I really quite enjoy my time so far at this school'.

'On my first day at school the place was so big and the teachers looked so angry I did not want to come again but the school has shrunk and the teachers are not so angry and I enjoy every day here'.

'When I walked through the doors I smelt the cared-for smell of polish. I wondered whether I would care for this school or this school would care for me'.

'The grounds are lovely and cover a wide space of land. When you are driving into school the fields behind the school of daffodils look lovely'.

'The school and its surroundings are beautiful, especially in the morning'.

'When I first came to St Swithun's I thought that it was quite an ordinary school but I soon found this wasn't true. To start with, there's five hundred dogs roaming about and every time I meet one of them they walk into me or even run when they're on the games pitch. In fact sometimes when the dogs are together it looks like there are more dogs in the school than girls'.

'There is a happy atmosphere at school and most people seem to get on well with each other. Most people enjoy having all the sports facilities like six grass courts, one indoor court and nine hard courts. The sports hall has been very popular and especially the new idea of a Tuck shop this term. I think it is good to have other activities like photography, computer club and art club.'

'I think one of the nicest ideas is the collecting of teachers. At the beginning of term you volunteer to be a teacher's monitress. Then at the lesson she teaches you wait for her outside the staff room. When she comes out you ask to carry her books and escort her to the lesson, chatting, hopefully, all the way. At the moment my greatest wish is to be leader of the first orchestra. My second greatest wish is to know what the staff room looks like.'

'This is my first school that the food has been jolly good and I can sit down and enjoy it for once. The thing that annoys me is that the queue is always so long and as I am a Lower IV all the other girls push in front and I don't have the courage to say "I was here before you" so I have to wait longer for lunch.'

'One of the first things I liked was the lunch hour. One early lunch a week was a super idea instead of queueing up for every lunch. After lunch I found I could do whatever I wanted. Sometimes I go to the library to read or play chess, on other days I go and play games on the computers and on Wednesday (our early lunch) we go to the sports hall to play tennis or any other game we want. On any other day we can play table tennis in the gallery whenever we like.'

'I like St Swithun's most of all because it is not forming its girls into soft gentle creatures but girls who are hardy and slightly extrovert that grow up with the continual thought in the back of their minds, never give up however dire the circumstances might be.'

A Sixth-form view

'A glance from the Alresford Road at the imposing exterior of St Swithun's as it stands today on its commanding site above Winchester, convinces us immediately of the praiseworthy design of its planners, founders and patrons; it cannot, however, convey more than a very superficial impression of the quality and flavour of a life which, in term-time at least, flourishes within those walls. For here there exists a world in microcosm which is undoubtedly best experienced, if not always appreciated at the time, by donning that familiar brown uniform and advancing through its portals at a relatively early age.

I took this step in my twelfth year on a day which I remember almost as clearly as my last day at St Swithun's seven years later. The building seemed to be a maze of long corridors and echoing wooden staircases, and, with its own grounds, garden and swimming pool, reminded me of a small metropolis which housed then, and continues to house, a surprisingly complete little community, of which each year forms a distinct unit, its members acquiring, I observed, a greater individuality and identity as they progress through school.

The stress on encouraging as many girls as possible to step, in their spare time at school, beyond the academic tramlines in search of a wider range of interests, has always seemed to me to be one of the key features of life at St Swithun's. Each of the clubs begun and fostered to promote a talent for music, drama, sport, photography, cookery, art, religious discussion and so on, was, I realised, aimed at giving us the opportunity to widen our range of leisure activities. Thus, while mixing with girls from different academic stages in the school, broadening our horizons and making new friends, we were enabled to develop a well rounded personality, surely the ultimate goal of a complete education.

Not, of course, that life at St Swithun's is merely one giddy round of dramatic presentations, concerts, matches, music recitals and the like; we are primarily here to work—academic qualifications being an undeniable asset to the school leaver especially in these times of rising unemployment. The community spirit mentioned earlier applies here too, within the classroom, coming to its fruition as one enters the VIth form, beginning one's chosen subjects in a relationship with the teaching staff that is suddenly more mature and much more fulfilling, if more demanding, for both parties. I derived a great sense of security and stability from this, being encouraged by the very personal interest that the staff showed in my work and character as a whole.

We all responded to the challenge, at this stage, of being expected to play an active role in the day-to-day running of the school. One might be forgiven for thinking that repeatedly ordering a recalcitrant member of the Upper IVth to scrape her lunch plate properly before placing it on the dining room trolley, or trying to limit the voracious Middle Vth to only two school biscuits each during the morning break, would make little favourable impression on one's "whole personality", but I found the simple discipline required in remembering to do the task at all was of some value. So too one gains self confidence and a greater sense of responsibility from involvement in planning the many varied house activities, my own interest in the social services taking me outside the school in search of children's homes eager for sweets at Christmas and elderly people who were willing to be visited.

St Swithun's, like so many institutions, has its official and its unofficial face—I recall the annual school Confirmations, the awed silence, almost palpable in the Cathedral's chilly vaults; the sea of white faces, the swish of our choir cloaks as we step down the aisles. I feel again the candlelit serenity of a school evensong, and the intimacy of a private school Communion when the Bramston Hall becomes, for a few hours, a sacred chapel, its floors, pounded by yesterday's eager (and not so eager) gymnasts and by the tangled and giggling sets of Scottish dancers on rainy days, brushed now by the white cloth of the Altar and by the feet of the youngsters trying not to fidget.

Here too are those days in mid-summer when all our familiar old desks and favourite little nooks are swept clean and turned quite upside down in the preparation for the annual opening of the school to our parents: patient fathers are dragged once more around all those fascinating experiments in the chemistry and biology labs, to the hearty family tennis tournament, and to keen competition from other fathers in the domestic science department's energetic scone or shortbread-making competition, the mothers to the madrigal recitals, the art exhibitions, and the project displays, before being led exhausted up to the dining room for tea. The concerts too, with dry-mouthed soloists backstage, generally somewhat more reticent than their contemporaries in the chorus who will talk quite merrily about anything and everything, to the exasperation of those charged with the task of keeping them quiet, right up to the moment for the throwing aside their combs and advancing into the bright lights of the hall.

Yet for each of these official functions, so carefully prepared or rehearsed, there is an informal celebration, in which only members of the school could ever share: end of term excitement reaches fever pitch during the half hour or so devoted to the pupils' Gaudy—the lusty yelling of traditional songs, accompanied, usually rather feebly, on the piano, and punctuated by stamps, shouts and the waving of streamers, all vaguely intended to correspond to the rhythm of the piece. The festivities end with an emotional rendering of 'Auld Lang Syne' for which the Headmistress, very nobly I think, in view of the volume of the noise that must by this time have penetrated the staff room, picks her way through the throng to join in.

Another end-of-term favourite, sadly but understandably rare, and consequently all the more precious, is the staff play—a delicious spoof, in the performing of which every participant soars in the popularity ratings, simply through willingness to take an irreverent look at school life. The fact that the headmistress is able to appear in just such a performance as The Old Woman Who Lived In A Shoe, or rather a Lacrosse Boot (surrounded, as you may have guessed, by her many children) provoking shrieks of laughter and bursts of applause from the audience, yet still continue to command the degree of respect appropriate to her position in the school, is, I feel, ample proof of the success of St Swithun's community spirit as a whole, and the personal attitude upon which it rests.

Each departure from the routine school week is treasured and appreciated to the full: few, I think, will forget the weeks when the irrepressible catering staff treated us to a gastronomic tour of the world—the American-style hamburgers, French crêpes, Italian pasta dishes of every description, and British baked potatoes with a choice of fillings, nor could one overlook the week they promoted fish dishes, complete with sou'westers and plastic ducks, or the amazing collection of hats they sport each Christmas.

Such moments of hilarity swelled by the many little pranks nobly suffered as a predictable feature of the closing term, are balanced by the order of the academic curriculum and the discipline of the lacrosse pitch or tennis court. There are many for whom those spirited encounters out on the turf and the challenge of working as a team in competition with others of similar interests is a very important part of school life. With such great choice of sporting activities now on offer at St Swithun's there are few, if any, who cannot find something to their taste, and I am grateful to the staff concerned for recognising my physical limitations and humouring my efforts on the field, however inept.

No portrait of St Swithun's would be complete without some mention of the final year in Finlay, the house shared by the boarders and day girls of the upper VIth and intended by its designers as a bridge between one's time at school and the next stage in life, whatever that may be. How I shall miss the chaos of the tiny Finlay kitchen crammed with ten or eleven other sixth formers all trying to make those endless pieces of toast and cups of coffee which become indispensable to the writing of 'A' level essays. How I shall miss running across the common room to seize a cushion for those few summer afternoons spent on the terrace, the companionship of our shared day studies and our idle conversation over the daily papers. Yet these were the luxuries granted for a year which seemed to pass all too quickly, dominated as it was by thoughts of the future. 'A' levels loomed ever nearer as text books began to accumulate in ever-increasing heaps and files groaned under the weight of expanding notes. The process of facing that daunting mass of U.C.C.A. forms, those applications for secretarial colleges and nursing courses, all the choices and decisions to be made, was greatly eased and speeded by consultation with the subject and careers staff, whose concern extended, on occasions, as far as waiting anxiously outside examination rooms to receive the comments of the emerging candidates.

And so another school year comes to an end and another upper VIth departs forever, each member taking the next stride out on their chosen path, as the school closes for the long summer holidays.'

Portraits

. (*above*) Miss Mowbray
. (*above right*) Miss Finlay
. (*below*) Miss Watt

4. Miss Evans

5. Miss Davies

6. The present Council

7. School 1900

8. The original Earlsdown

Buildings and Interiors

9. Aerial photograph 1983

10. - 13. Four interiors, High House 1900

ree interiors, school houses, 1983

. (*opposite page, above*) Study Bedroom - Finlay House
. (*opposite page, below*) Piano Room
. (*above*) Computer Study

Events

17.   Miss Mowbray's silver jubilee, 1910

18. Cutting the first sod, 1930

19. Laying the foundation stone of the new school

20. - 22. Opening of the new school, 1933, by the Princess Royal

23. - 26. The Duchess of Gloucester attends the 75th anniversary

Personalities

27. (*above*) Miss Bramston and Miss Leroy
28. (*left*) Miss Bramston in 1930
29. (*opposite page, above*) The Staff, 1886
30. (*opposite page, below*) The Sixth form, 18

Games   31. Hockey, 1897

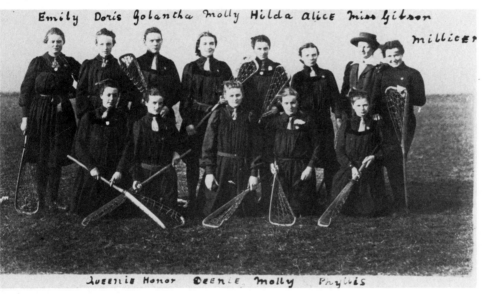

Emily Doris Golantha Molly Hilda Alice Miss Gibson

Millicent

Queenie Honor Deenie Molly Phyllis

32. (*top*) Cricket, 1950s
33. (*centre*) Lacrosse team, 1910
34. (*bottom*) Lacrosse team, Merton tournament, 1979

(*above*) Judo, 1970s
(*below*) Gym, 1980

37. Swimming, 1978

38. Junior School Gym, 1980s

sure

(*top right*) Riding lesson, 1906
(*centre*) Starting for school, 1906
(*bottom right*) Seniors, 1906. D.
(seated on right) was to be maths
s for 30 years

42. (*above*) Starting for Avington 1904
43. (*centre*) Picnic at Avington 1907
44. (*below*) Old Girls visiting in 1905

High House Garden, 1930s
Juniors, 1950s

and 48. 1979 Celmi

49. 1981 Easter cruise on SS *Uganda*

50. Sponsored walk, 1970

ademic

right) Art studio (old)
below) Art studio (new)
bottom right) Library (old)
bottom left) Library (new)

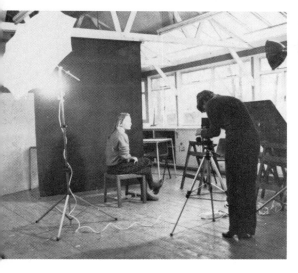

55. Orchestra (old)
56. Orchestra (new)

57. Sixth form room (old)

58. Sixth form room (new)

59. - 62. Four classrooms in the 1950s

63.   The main staircase and the honours boards

Drama

64. (*above left*) *The Taming of the Shrew*,
1930s
65. (*above right*) Charlotte Yonge
charades, 1890s
66. (*centre*) *The Immortal Lady*, 1951
67. (*below*) *Charlie and the Chocolate
Factory*, 1980

68. and 69.   The Winchester Pageant, 1908

70. and 71.   Greek dancing, 1928

Behind the Scenes

Seen from the Staff Room

'I have been at St Swithun's so long that I suppose one would expect a whole host of memories and tales of the doings of girls and staff and the changes I have seen. But, strangely, I don't really find it easy to think of separate times and events, and in any case they are recorded elsewhere. For my own part, I look through these years and find the whole leaves an impression with me of belonging to a sort of family and a very supportive one at that. I have revelled in being part of this thriving, caring, exuberant family where I know when I go to work I am going to enjoy every day; well, nearly every day.

The teaching for me is two-way, from girls to staff as well as the other way round. The emphasis, built up over all my years here, but particularly in the last ten to fifteen years, has certainly been on academic achievement, and I continue to be impressed and surprised by the amount of really hard work put in by most girls. This, of course, means that the staff work very hard to meet their needs and we always work for each girl and not just for the class as a whole. In my own subject I seem to have been teaching myself something new or, if not new, more advanced, in mathematics the whole time, and I begin to think no level of advanced maths would be too high for gifted girls of about seventeen or eighteen. They seem to lap it up. But equally I see more and more that the less academic girl is learning something so worthwhile here, enough to give her confidence to go off and carve out a really impressive career. The 'Old Girls' news is extremely good reading, and I get no better at guessing at the true potential of some of these girls. Clever or not, they can look quite meek and ordinary sitting at a desk trying to do their maths, but in the evenings you sometimes meet them in the Houses acting a sophisticated and charming hostess role and then later on one reads that they have travelled the world, risen to the top of a profession, probably married and had several children as well, and all this seems to happen in no time at all. I have had to get used to teaching the children of children I taught, extra interest this, and I really do not share the common view that children have changed. These little girls seem uncannily like their Mamas.

My own job is fascinatingly varied. I spend a good deal of time hurrying around with bits of paper in my hand, trying to look important, but I never know what will crop up next. Every day is different. Little re-organisation jobs, necessary because someone is away or some class is off on an expedition, never pick their times to suit me, it seems. The Staff Room 'phone ringing about 8.30 a.m. usually means some minor disruption of the routine day and I find that on the day it rings once it is inclined to get over-fond of the exertion, like an excited dog who seems just to have discovered how to bark. Some days an assortment of girls or staff will wander into my little room to tell me their troubles. One day recently, when the headmistress was away, I had to receive a rather eminent and entirely unexpected guest to coffee only to discover he had come to the wrong school. I have to field recurring grumbles from all departments ranging from salt mixed with pepper by some boring little horror in the dining room, to classrooms left too dirty to clean, or even the headmistress up against some problem she wants to share. Well it is great to feel needed, everyone deserves that. And then there is always the teaching. Once inside the classroom I feel reasonably safe and the girls marvellous at gauging my mood and adjusting theirs wisely to accord with it.

It is really a lovely life. You have to like childen and hard work I suppose, but the mixture here of lively, intelligent girls and friends among the staff (teaching, offices and catering staff), who could not be bettered, have been the framework for most of my working years and I think luck was most certainly on my side when I applied for a job at St Swithun's back in 1955.'

From the P.E. Department

'At present with the school's centenary in view, recollection and reminiscence are all around us, and it is impossible not to compare present day at school with St Swithun's as it was even, say, twenty five years ago. Everyone wore hats in those days—summer "beehives", winter felt, or a beret if you rode your bicycle. You wore your house tie (no purse belts) with your tailored "skirt" suit or on Friday, before Saturday's matches, you wore your lacrosse tie, or your swimming tie instead of your house tie. In the summer of course, you could not wear your match tie round your neck, so with great care and pride, you suspended it from the belt of your dress.

Earlsdown, Hillcroft, Chilcomb (boarding houses) and LeRoy all rushed back down the hill every day for lunch—seniors on bicycles and juniors on feet. Juniors always started afternoon school a few minutes later than the main school because of the walk.

Hillcroft and Earlsdown used to have "posture" lunches once a week when inspections were the order of the day. Not a head drooped, nor a spine quivered. All members of Earlsdown had two ties, one for everyday and one for posture lunch, and that tie was very grubby—a result of trying to accomplish the near-impossible feat of transporting food from table to mouth with a spine like a ramrod.

Things seemed to be very much more clear-cut in those days. Now the edges are blurred and the lines bent. Fashions have changed—and a good thing too. Games shorts were half an inch from the floor when kneeling, and were worn winter and summer. Absolutely no-one ever wore a tennis skirt, but when the sun came out you were despatched with all possible haste indoors to fetch your white cricket hat. *And you wore it*!

A few years ago, the swimming season really was short and it is only comparatively recently that we have had any heating in the pool at all. No-one went swimming until the water temperature registered 60°F. for three consecutive days. It rarely did this, of course, so when we were tired of waiting we cheated, and everyone went in willy nilly. At that end of the scale, one's big toe was scarcely able to differentiate between 59°F. and 60°F.

Nowadays very few girls come to this school as non-swimmers. A few years ago, there were quite a number, but no-one ever left St Swithun's as a non-swimmer.

We have undergone a startling metamorphosis during the past twelve months with the building of the Sports Hall. Before that, we must go back to the re-building of the junior school for any major development. 'Elephant House' (J.S. gym) was made large enough to accommodate one first class badminton court. Other than that, two new hard courts were newly laid sometime in the early 1960s, I think.

Nowadays the time table is flexible in a way it never was twenty five years ago. In those days all swimming took place in the mornings, and all games in the afternoons (and evenings in the summer, 4.20-6.20). Indoor and outdoor lessons are mixed now, so that one could equally well find oneself playing badminton or lacrosse, or having a gym lesson first thing on a Monday morning. Middle Vth upwards all learn badminton and there is a wide choice of activity for the Upper Vth and VIth forms—archery, golf, self-defence, keep fit and netball, as well as lacrosse, tennis and swimming. The Fencing section continues to flourish and there is always a large following for Judo.

The school grows and flourishes strongly, although still very firmly rooted in its traditions, and the fine things in its past. In attitude it largely reflects the changes and relaxations to be found in any modern institution or community, and within a framework of easier discipline, there really is a remarkably friendly and relaxed atmosphere in the school.'

But the last word of all must lie with Miss Davies who brought fresh honour to herself and to the school when she was chosen as President of the Girls School Association for the year 1981-82. This office gave her the fullest opportunity to observe the state of Girls' Independent education at the beginning of the 1980s, and to relate it to the present needs of St Swithun's.

From the Headmistress

' "The ideal presented to a young girl is to be amiable, inoffensive, always ready to give pleasure, and to be pleased . . . There is a long-established and inveterate prejudice that girls are less capable of mental cultivation and less in need of it than boys; that accomplishments and what is showy and superficially attractive are what is really essential".

So said Emily Davies, a pioneer of education for girls when in 1864 she gave evidence at the Schools' Inquiry Commission under the chairmanship of Lord Taunton.

Twenty years later St Swithun's School was founded, though under the cumbersome name of Winchester Diocesan High School for Girls. It was part of a growing movement which recognized that the intellect of half the population was being neglected, if not deliberately suppressed.

St Swithun's played no small part in the national movement for the education of girls. The Association of Headmistresses was formed in 1874 by Miss Frances Mary Buss and it is recorded that Miss Mowbray, headmistress of Winchester High School, was one of the Headmistresses who attended the first formal conference at Uppingham in 1887. Twelve years later she was appointed Chairman of the Committee. The early pioneers were women of courage, determination and tireless energy and in the latter end of the 20th century it is difficult to appreciate the prejudice that had to be overcome.

The battle was won. Education became compulsory for all, but it is only in the last decade or so that real equality of opportunity has been established. The last 15 years has seen as dramatic a surge forward in girls' education as that of the late 19th century. Women are increasingly seeking posts of responsibility in a variety of careers that were traditionally reserved for men. It is no longer a matter of surprise to parents that their daughters wish to take University courses in engineering, medicine, computer studies or any of the pure sciences, and a flurry of building and expenditure on scientific equipment in girls' schools was a marked feature of the late '60s and early '70s.

But recognition of potential and equal opportunity does not necessarily lead to fulfilment. The greater the opportunities the more problems it poses and the responsibilities of choice become more pressing.

In the 1880s, as in the 1980s, the monarch was a Queen, but it would have been unthinkable then that her Government could have been led by a woman Prime Minister. The Victorian age produced some remarkable women, mainly concerned with educational and social reform but against a background where, for the majority, a career was regarded as a second-best alternative to marriage.

Fifty years ago, the curriculum in girls' grammar and independent schools was little more than an imitation of that offered for boys. The Education Act of 1944 started a breakthrough towards greater breadth of choice but it took a second world war to change the social attitudes towards women with career ambitions. Even then, it was a slow and gradual process. Educated to the same level of achievement as men at school and university or other forms of higher education, the Victorian alternatives of career or marriage still persisted. This was the dilemma of the mid-20th century. Earlier marriage and better living conditions left a vacuum for women when their children had become independent and it was in the affluent '60s that they were given wider opportunities to continue where they had left off. Universities expanded and higher education for girls was increasingly accepted and expected. Education is more a reflector than a trend-setter of social conditions and girls' schools expanded their curriculum to meet the increased demand.

But have we come full circle? In the 1980s the intellectual capability of women is not in question and the 'role of women' is no longer clearly defined. It is possible that this lack of clarity is the dilemma of the late 20th century which will be resolved by educationalists in succeeding years. Girls in schools do not now anticipate a clear-cut choice between career and marriage. They now have a multi-role as bearers of children, home-makers, career specialists in their own right and contributors to the family budget. They are financially independent and independence brings responsibilities of a different kind.

The Victorian battles fought for the education of girls have finally been won, but victory has brought other problems in its wake. Recognition of intellectual ability is not enough if conditions still exist which make it difficult of fulfilment.

Today's schoolgirls will probably work throughout their lives—some of them having a two-part life with a break for child-rearing. They will face challenges, stresses, joys and compromises which they will have to meet for themselves. In working out the solutions, the understanding of the problems and preparation for meeting them provides a new exciting prospect for girls' schools in the 1980s, and is one to which St Swithun's is well equipped to contribute.'

Appendix

The first school ledger has survived, giving information about the first girls at the school, who were: G. Bird, G. Butcher, P. Chevalier, D. Clark, A. K. Cornish, H. du Boulay, B. du Boulay, M. Frazer, M. French, A. French, A. Gale, G. Kirby, D. Knight, M. Moberly, A. Stopher, R. Stopher and E. Ward. The ledger also provides the names of their parents, and it is, perhaps, of interest to list their occupations where it has been possible to identify them, to see just how much of a 'social mix' there was in the early days.

Robert Bird was a local lawyer and E. Butcher a hatter and furrier at 33 High Street, Winchester. P. Chevalier's father was a clergyman, as was the du Boulays father, who was probably the son of the Rev. James du Boulay, one of the first Housemasters of the College. R. C. Gale was a surveyor, J. F. Kirby was bursar at the College and Captain Knight a local landowner. A. E. Moberly was a descendant of George Moberly, Headmaster of the College, 1836-1866. W. Stopher was an ironmonger of 11a Jewry Street, Winchester, while G. Ward was a grocer and poulterer of 66-67 High Street, Winchester.

During the first year, when numbers rose to 48, the following further identification among parents can be made: from the College, E. J. Turner and T. Kensington, both Housemasters; from the professions, W. Bowker, W. Shenton and Mr. Scotney, all lawyers, with Alfred Edmeades, their managing clerk, T. C. Langdon, a doctor, W. Coles, the Borough Engineer and Mr. Knapp, a banker. Among the local business people were R. Hunt, chemist, and Mr. Hayward of Haywards General Store at the corner of High Street and Southgate Street, Winchester. Mr. Whitaker of Pywell Park was a landowner, at one time High Sheriff and Chairman of the Trustees of St Cross Hospital.

Among those who were either debenture holders or who gave donations to the Capital Fund were a large number of local clergy, including the Dean, Archdeacons Atkinson (who became the first chairman) and Jacob, and Canons Bridges, Humbert, le Mesurier, Mosby Lee and Muspratt. The College, too, gave its support: the Warden the Rev. G. B. Lee, the Headmaster W. A. Fearon, Housemasters C. H. Hawkins, C. B. Phillips and A. J. Toye and from the Staff, E. D. A. Morshead. Contributions from local business and trading interests included Wyndham Portal, the owner of paperworks at Haverstock, J. Pamplin, owner of a bookshop and an hotel in Godbegot House, W. T. Warren, a stationer and printer and owner of the *Hampshire Observer*, Mr. Parmiter who ran the Post Office and was a wine and spirit merchant, and T. Lloyd who had an ironmonger's business.

The school accounts for the first year show that donations amounted to £276 19s., loans on debenture to £300 and scholars' fees to £537 19s. The total receipts were £1,114 18s. Expenditure amounted to £956 0s. 5d., leaving a balance of £149 17s 7d.

Index